THE PRIMACY OF PETER

Thou art Peter, and it is upon this rock
that I will build my Church. . . . *Where then
have Christ's words to Peter produced a
corresponding effect except in the chair
of Peter? Where does that chair find
adequate cause except in the promise made
to Peter?*

SOLOVIEV

Simon, son of John . . . feed my lambs . . . feed my
sheep . . . feed my sheep. . . . *These words of the
Savior, repeated three times just before He
ascended into heaven, are truly like the
mantle which Elias threw to Eliseus.*

ROSANOV

THE PRIMACY
OF PETER

From the Protestant and from the Catholic Point of View

MONSIGNOR CHARLES JOURNET

Translated from the French by John Chapin

THE NEWMAN PRESS   *Westminster, Maryland*
1954

Nihil obstat: Eduardus A. Cerny, S.S., D.D.
        Censor Librorum

Imprimatur: Franciscus P. Keough, D.D.
        Archiepiscopus Baltimorensis

die 4 mensis Octobris, 1954

The *nihil obstat* and *imprimatur* are official declarations that a book or pamphlet is free of doctrinal and moral error. No implication is contained therein that those who have granted the *nihil obstat* and *imprimatur* agree with the opinions expressed.

CONTENTS

INTRODUCTION

My intention to devote a short work entirely to a discussion of the principal arguments of *Peter, Disciple, Apostle, Martyr* [1] may be interpreted as an indication of my high regard both for the book and for its author, Oscar Cullmann, Professor at the University of Basel and at the École des Hautes-Études, Sorbonne, Paris. For the points which he makes relate to the most obvious, if not the most serious, controversial issue which separates Protestants and Catholics.

Prof. Cullmann invites Catholics and Protestants to

---

[1] Oscar Cullmann, *Pierre, disciple, apôtre, martyr: Histoire et théologie* (Neuchâtel, 1952), 230 pp. This is the French version of a work which was originally published in German: *Petrus, Jünger, Apostel, Märtyrer* (Zurich, 1952). It has also been translated into English by Floyd V. Filson: *Peter, Disciple, Apostle, Martyr: a Historical and Theological Study* (Philadelphia: The Westminster Press, 1952), 252 pp.

discuss these points at issue among themselves. He writes in the foreword to his work:

> Indeed, we promote mutual and improved understanding only if we do not pass over in silence that which separates us. Where men, fully aware that they invoke the same name, make a sincere effort to listen to one another, they need not fear to speak also concerning the themes on which, as far as human eye can see, agreement is not possible. I often note, in discussions between representatives of the various confessions, that both parties take anxious pains to speak only concerning those questions regarding which there exists a common basis of discussion. The other questions are studiously avoided, even though as a rule the conversation necessarily reaches a point where it should move on to precisely those other questions for which the common basis is lacking. When this point is reached, one should go back to the reason for this lack of a common basis, not —let me repeat—to fight for one's position and not, indeed, with the illusory purpose of converting one's partner, but rather to listen to him.[2]

This is precisely what I intend to do here in discussing one of those themes on which agreement between Protestantism and Catholicism is impossible. Two comments, however, need to be made on the passage which has just been read. In the first place, once we decide to leave out of the picture the great mass of liberal Protes-

---

[2] Cullmann, *Peter, Disciple, Apostle, Martyr*, pp. 11-12. (All references are to the English version of Prof. Cullmann's work, and are used with the permission of the publishers, The Westminster Press, Philadelphia, Pa. According to the translator, this version was prepared in close collaboration with Prof. Cullmann himself. In a few instances it has seemed advisable to include the French version of a phrase or two when there appeared to be a slight difference in emphasis, because the French version is the one which Msgr. Journet himself quotes and on which his comments are based. —Translator's note.)

tants and confine our conversation to that portion of Protestantism which is willing to acknowledge the divinity of Christ and some kind of divine inspiration for Holy Scripture, we believe that there is a "common basis" between them and ourselves, namely Christ and the Scriptures. It is up to the reader to decide between two ways of understanding the mystery of Jesus, between two ways of reading the Gospels, the one Protestant and the other Catholic; it would amount to an oversimplification of the issues to oppose Protestantism and Catholicism by giving the reader his choice, between Christ and the Gospel as representative of Protestantism on the one hand, and the Church and its teaching office as representative of Catholicism on the other hand. Finally, would it be worth while to expose the differences between Catholicism and Protestantism for the sole purpose of "listening" to each other? That would certainly not be enough from our point of view. Must we not give thought to the young who still have a choice to make, and to those still uncommitted adult minds which are searching for the truth like a spring in the desert and are capable of overcoming all kinds of fatal obstacles in their path in order to attain it? Must we not think of them when we write and speak? "When you enter this house, you are to wish it well. . . ." (Matt. X, 12-15)[3] Besides, could one be a true follower of Augustine or Thomas Aquinas if he did not feel that every occasion when a truth is questioned ought to be used for the purpose of throwing more light on it and bearing witness each day in a less imperfect way to the reve-

[3] The scriptural references are from the *New Testament* in the translation of Msgr. Ronald Knox, copyright 1944 by Sheed & Ward, Inc., New York.

lation which daily seems to be more and more ineffable? I refer here again to some of the statements of the great theologians of the sixteenth century, cited in my work *The Church of the Word Incarnate*,[4] which assist us to explain the problem of the primacy of Saint Peter as it appears in the light of the Gospels, and try to make their meaning more explicit. How can I fail to express my gratitude at this point to that humble and penetrating genius of an interpreter of Saint Thomas, to whom the Popes of the sixteenth century appealed for theological explanations about all the various points in dispute at the time, Cardinal Cajetan?

No one recalled the fact that the Pope is the supreme head of the Church with respect to jurisdiction more ably than he. No one more ably recalled at the same time that the order of jurisdiction, necessary and even divine as it is, is not what is best and most divine in the Church, but derives all its greatness from the fact that it is meant to serve the purpose of love. According to Cajetan:

> Peter is the minister of the Church; not because it is superior to him in power, but because he uses his power to serve it. Did the Lord himself not say that he had come in order to serve? When the Pope declares that he is the servant of the servants of God, he declares the truth. But the Church is greater and better than the Pope, as the end is greater and better than that which exists for it; according to Saint Augustine, to be greater means to be better in the qualitative order. The papacy exists for the sake of the Church, not vice versa. It is therefore true that the Pope is not the master but the servant, and that the Church, absolutely speaking, surpasses him in goodness

[4] Charles Journet, *L'Eglise du Verbe incarné* (Paris, 1941-53), 2 volumes.

and nobility, although in the sphere of jurisdiction he is its head.[5]

At the very beginning of the present work, which will henceforth be concerned only with the jurisdictional primacy of Peter, we wish to declare the absolute primacy of the order of charity over the order of jurisdiction. It is because charity is so divine that it requires to be divinely directed from outside, and it is precisely to the extent that jurisdiction is divine that it may seek to direct divine charity. The end of jurisdictional power and sacramental power is to give to charity the possibility of being sacramental and directed, of being fully Christlike, and of becoming the created soul of the Church which shapes the whole body from within.

By emphasizing at the same time both the primacy of Peter in the jurisdictional order and the primacy of the order of charity over the order of jurisdiction, Cajetan follows his master Saint Thomas in pointing out that in addition to the pastoral responsibility of insisting at a given moment on this or that aspect of revealed truth which happens to be misunderstood or threatened at a given time, as the dialectic of controversy or history may suggest, the Church is continually concerned at the same time to carry out its teaching responsibility of asserting all the complementary aspects of this indivisible truth. There is always a danger for Christianity when one of these two responsibilities of the Church temporarily lacks a voice with which to express itself. The concern for immediate needs and the concern for larger considerations, which appears, for example, at an ecu-

[5] Cajetan, *Apologia de comparata auctoritate papae et concilii* (Edit. Pollet), no. 517.

menical council, are two aspects of the teaching responsibility of the Church, the royal and the prophetic.

No attempt will be made here to discuss critically the valuable suggestions of Prof. Cullmann which should be of interest to the Biblical exegete and the historian of the origins of Christianity, nor to list the numerous rewarding passages which are to be found in this clearly written, sincere, and learned work. I have only attempted to oppose two different points of view as clearly as possible, on behalf of which the same facts and the same texts can be alleged. If the mystery of the Incarnation is true, if it is true that God so loved the world that he gave his only-begotten Son, if the Word was made flesh, if he watches each day until the end of time over the revelation he once made to the world, if the Gospel is more than an historical document and is a living and perpetual mystery of faith and love, the point of view which reveals its fullest, most mysterious and most divine meaning is the one in my opinion which is the only true meaning.

Fribourg, February 10, 1953

THE PRIMACY OF PETER

1

SUMMARY OF PROF.
CULLMANN'S BOOK

When discussing the exegetical method of Alfred Loisy, Father Gardeil wrote fifty years ago:

> It seems to me that the Catholic theologian must choose between two methods: one is the *historical* or *progressive* method, constructing theology from a primitive datum, from origins such as they appear in the documentary sources; the other is the *regressive* method, starting from the historical terminus of a traditional evolutionary process, regarded as something established, in order to go back from there to the sources.[1]

He illustrated his thought by citing the probable account of two explorers who were looking for the sources of the Congo; one of them methodically traced the river to its origin; the other, in order to get there more quick-

[1] Ambroise Gardeil, O.P., "L'Idee d'une methode regressive," *Revue thomiste* (1903), p. 19.

ly, started from Zanzibar, reached the watershed, and discovered . . . the sources of the Nile!

The regressive method is the one every true theologian instinctively follows; it guides and directs him, even if he decides to deal with documents in a chronological order. In spite of the fact that he intends to write primarily a historical study, as he himself says, there can be no doubt that Prof. Cullmann is writing more often as a theologian than he is as a philologist or an exegete. But the starting point from which he goes back to clarify his exegesis of the New Testament is a Protestant concept of the Church which is no longer that of the Reformation or of Barthism, or that of liberal individualism, but which approximates in some respects views widely held in the Church of England.

There can only be praise for this work if one takes into account the massive learning which is displayed, the perfect clarity of its arrangement, and the unquestionable constant integrity of its argumentation. In spite of the richness of the material contained therein, it is easy to summarize the work without altering the sense, because the author has himself taken care to summarize each of its parts.

The historical section, in which he treats Peter successively as a disciple, apostle, and martyr, occupies the major portion of the work:

> In summary of our entire historical section, to the end of which we now have come, we must say that during the life time of Peter he held a pre-eminent position among the disciples; that after Christ's death he presided over the church at Jerusalem in the first years; that he then became the leader of the Jewish Christian mission; that in this capacity, at a time which cannot be more closely

determined but probably occurred at the end of his life, he came to Rome and there, after a very short work, died as a martyr under Nero.[2]

Then follows an exegetical study of Matthew, XVI, 17-19:

Our exegetical study has led us to the following result: The saying in Matthew, XVI, 17ff. is genuine. It was spoken by Jesus, not at Caesarea Philippi, but in another setting, possibly that of the passion story. Jesus promises Peter that he will build upon him the earthly people [French Version: temple] of God that will lead to the Kingdom of God; he promises that in this people Peter will have the leadership, both in missionary work and in organization. His immediate thought, just as in John, XXI, 16ff., probably deals only with the time of Peter. But even if he explicitly had in view the period following Peter's death as the time of the building of the Church, what is said of Peter as the Rock refers only to him, the historical apostle; he represents once for all the earthly foundation, the beginning which supports the whole structure of the *ekklesia* that is to be built in the future.[3]

Finally, the doctrinal discussion leads to the following conclusions:

In so far as Peter is the Rock, he is such in the temporal sense of laying the foundation as an apostle. In every generation Christ intends to build his Church on the founda-

2 Cullmann, *Peter, Disciple, Apostle, Martyr*, p. 152. (The French version has the additional words, ". . . probably as a result of difficulties which arose between the Jewish-Christian and pagan-Christian elements in the capital," immediately following ". . . in this capacity."—Translator's note.)

3 *Ibid.*, pp. 211-212. (The French version has at the end, ". . . who represents once for all the earthly foundation of the *ekklesia* still to be built, the first stone which will support all the others."—Translator's note.)

tion of the apostles, and among them Peter is the most important.

In so far as he is the leader of the Primitive Church in Jerusalem, this also has chiefly temporal significance, and in this respect his bearing for the redemptive history of all later time consists in the fact that he held the leadership of the original Church.

If we wish to derive further from the saying that after Peter also there must be in the Church a universal leadership that administers the keys, the power to bind and loose, this cannot take place in the sense of a limitation to the future occupants of one episcopal see. This principle of succession cannot be justified either from Scripture or from the history of the ancient Church. In reality the leadership of the Church at large is not to be determined by succession in the sense of a link with one episcopal see. The significance of individual churches for the Church at large comes and goes. But the Rock, the foundation for all Churches of all times, remains the historical Peter. At that time he was especially chosen by Jesus from among the Twelve; he was given special distinction as a witness of Jesus' life and death and as the first witness of his resurrection. On him Christ, who is himself the cornerstone, will keep building his Church as long as there is such a Church on earth.[4]

In accordance with these views Prof. Cullmann is able to write on the very first page of his book the following sentences, consciously and deliberately mutilating each time the sense which they have for a Catholic:

"I believe in one holy catholic
and apostolic Church"

"You are 'Rock,' and on this Rock
I will build my Church" [Matt., XVI, 18]

4 Cullmann, *op. cit.*, pp. 237-238.

"Built upon the foundation of
the Apostles and Prophets" [Eph., II, 20]

"I pray for those who believe
through the word of the Apostles" [John, XVII, 20]

Our attention must now be directed to the way in
which the meaning is mutilated.

2

TWO IRRECONCILABLE CONCEPTS
OF CHRISTIANITY

There are two irreconcilable concepts of Christianity which are opposed to one another: one is the Catholic and Orthodox view; the other is that which lies at the basis of the various Protestant beliefs and which sometimes has a direct, strong influence on them, and sometimes only a rather remote, weakened influence.

Both claim to have the same starting point, Christ, true God and true Man, who once appeared on earth and has now returned to heaven. (I take no account here of the various forms of Protestantism which deny the divinity of Christ.) Both would agree in saying that the truly valid Christian experience involves a certain presence of Christ in the midst of men.

It is over the way in which this presence of Christ, which constitutes Christianity, is thought to exist in the midst of men that the two concepts differ. According to the first concept we must think of an *ontological* presence of Christ in Christianity, of a real and unbroken repercussion in time of a supremely important event which took place once and for all in the past, like a stone thrown into the water which gives rise to concentric waves which spread indefinitely through time and space. According to the second concept we must think only of a *mnemic presence* of Christ in Christianity, of the mere awareness through memory of an important event which took place once and for all in the past, like a meteorite which is consumed and leaves a trace only in our memory.

The *ontological concept* is that of a *realistic* form of Christianity, in that Christ truly and really is present in time under the guise of signs, tokens, and promises; as such, it appears as a sort of anticipation during this period of exile of the final home-coming: "The man who eats my flesh and drinks my blood enjoys eternal life, and I will raise him up at the last day" (John, VI, 55). "And if the spirit of him who raised up Jesus from the dead dwells in you, he who raised up Jesus Christ from the dead will give life to your perishable bodies too, for the sake of his Spirit who dwells in you" (Rom., VIII, 11).

The *mnemic concept* of Christianity is that of a *symbolical* kind of Christianity, in which Christ is only present in time by way of signs, tokens, and promises; as such, it appears from the Catholic point of view to be a sort of nostalgic form of the Old Testament. According to Saint Thomas, ". . . the state of the New Law is between the state of the Old Law, whose figures are fulfilled in the New, and the state of glory, in which all truth will be openly and perfectly revealed." [1] In the state of the Old Law the fulness was not yet present, but was foreshadowed under the form of signs or figures; in the state of the New Law the fulness is present, but is still hidden under the form of signs; in the state of glory the signs shall have disappeared.

Let us illustrate these two concepts by some examples.

[1] *The Summa of St. Thomas Aquinas,* III, Q. 61, a. 4, ad 1. Translated by Fathers of the English Dominican Province (3 vols.; New York: Benziger Brothers, Inc., 1947). Vol. II, p. 2355.

3

THE ONTOLOGICAL CONCEPT
OF CHRISTIANITY

1. THE HEAD AND THE BODY

According to this concept the origin of Christianity is marked by a unique impulse, a *hapax*, in Christ himself, who represents a unique and incomparable entry of eternity into time, the immediate counter-effect of which is the inauguration of a continuous presence of eternity in time in the Church, which is his body. These are the "last days" of which the Apostles speak, the last age of the history of the world, which is a preparation for the second coming of Christ in glory (*Parousia*) and the transfiguration of the world (*Apocatastasis*).

The Church is therefore like Christ; the Body is like the Head. This homogeneity of the Church with Christ, of the Body with the Head, enables Christ to be diffused and communicated in space and time. It assures a con-

tinuous presence of Christ in space and time. This is
the mystery of the Church's catholicity.

Once this perpetual and real presence of Christ in the
midst of space and time has been broken, once the continuity of the Christian mystery has been mutilated, the
desire to go on speaking of Catholicism and catholicity
at all costs amounts to nothing but insistence upon using
a traditional word which has been emptied of all traditional meaning.

2. THE CHURCH AS THE COMPLETION (PLEROMA) OF CHRIST

The basic notion of the inner superabundance of Christ,
actually being poured out in time to constitute the
Church, lies at the center of the New Testament revelation.

It sums up the teaching of Saint Paul, who declares
that God has put everything under the dominion of
Christ

> . . . and made him the head to which the whole Church
> is joined, so that the Church is his body, the completion
> [*pleroma*] of him who everywhere and in all things is
> complete (Eph., I, 22-23). He too is that head whose
> body is the Church; it begins with him, since his was the
> first birth out of death; thus in every way the primacy
> was to become his. It was God's good pleasure to let all
> completeness [*pleroma*] dwell in him, and through him
> to win back all things, whether on earth or in heaven,
> into union with himself, making peace with them through
> his blood, shed on the cross (Col., I, 18-20). In Christ
> the whole plenitude [*pleroma*] of Deity is embodied, and
> dwells in him, and it is in him that you find your comple-
> tion; he is the fountain head from which all dominion and
> power proceed (Col., II, 9-10).

Christ is the *pleroma* of Deity in the midst of us and
the Church is the *pleroma* of Christ. It completes Christ,
not intrinsically of course, but extrinsically. Hence Saint
Paul may write:

> . . . I help to pay off the debt which the afflictions of
> Christ leave still to be paid, for the sake of his body, the
> Church (Col., I, 24).

It also sums up the teaching of Saint John:

> And the Word was made flesh and came to dwell among
> us; and we had sight of his glory, glory such as belongs to
> the Father's only-begotten Son, full of grace and truth.
> . . . We have all received something of his abundance
> [*pleroma*], grace answering to grace (John, I, 14, 16).

There are two effusions, two births of eternal life in
time: one in Jesus; and the other in the Church, his
Body, his Spouse.

3. THE CHURCH IS CENTERED ON THE CORPORAL PRESENCE
   OF CHRIST IN TIME

The whole New Testament revelation is made clear in
the light of the view of the Church as the effusion of
Christ.

First of all, the Church in time continues to be centered on Christ who is present in the midst of it in time.
If God so loved the world that he gave his only-begotten
Son, will he love it enough to leave it this only-begotten
Son? If the bodily presence of his only-begotten Son has
been the center whence the salvation of the world has
sprung, is this same bodily presence going to be with-
drawn from us after the space of a mere thirty-three
years? Looking at things from the point of view of

divine love, I think we can be reasonably sure in advance that the earth will not be turned into a desert after Ascension Day. As a matter of fact, I find the following in Saint Paul:

> The tradition which I received from the Lord, and handed on to you, is that the Lord Jesus, on the night when he was being betrayed, took bread, and gave thanks, and broke it, and said, Take, eat; this is my body, which is to be given up for you. Do this for a commemoration of me. And so with the cup, when supper was ended, This cup, he said, is the new testament, in my blood. Do this, whenever you drink it, for a commemoration of me. So it is the Lord's death that you are heralding, whenever you eat this bread and drink this cup, until he comes; and therefore, if anyone eats this bread or drinks this cup of the Lord unworthily, he will be held to account for the Lord's body and blood (I Cor., XI, 23-27).

The Epistle to the Hebrews teaches that

> we have been sanctified by an offering made once and for all, the body of Jesus Christ. . . . By a single offering he has completed his work, for all time, in those whom he sanctifies (Heb., X, 10, 14).

The New Law is founded on Good Friday. The moment the sacrifice of redemption took place, the era of promise as such came to an end, and the era of fulfillment began. The presence of this sacrifice assures the world of unheard of riches, unknown in previous ages, when it was only offered symbolically and anticipated in faith. It is of such a nature that it brings about the salvation of all generations once and for all, but it can only communicate this to them successively, as they make their appearance in existence. In order to bring this about, it is of course not necessary that it be repeated, renewed, or multiplied (it is truly unique, perfect, and more than sufficient); what is necessary is that it be mysteriously present for each one of them—that is the special mystery of the Mass, which underlies every theological explanation—that it be extended to each one, as it were, for the purpose of attracting them into its orbit, bringing them its salutary virtue, permitting them to join in it as really and effectively as the primitive Church did, and finally for the purpose of inviting all Christians to share as members in the offering and fruits of the sacrifice of Christ, their Head.[1] The whole duration of historic time is thus made to form one coherent whole by the sacrifice of Calvary. Hence the words of Saint Paul when he contrasts the sacrificial meal of the first Christians with the sacrificial meals of the pagans:

> We have a cup that we bless; is not this cup we bless a participation in Christ's blood? Is not the bread we break a participation in Christ's body? The one bread makes us one body, though we are many in numbers; the same bread is shared by all. . . . To drink the Lord's cup, and yet to drink the cup of evil spirits, to share the Lord's feast, and to share the feast of evil spirits, is impossible for you (I Cor., X, 16, 21).

4. THE PERPETUATION OF CHRIST'S PRIESTHOOD AND KINGSHIP

Christ, as priest, inaugurates the worship of the new law on the Cross, and the presence of his priesthood, having completed its work once and for all, is to be

[1] See Charles Journet, *La sainte messe, ou la permanence du sacrifice de la loi nouvelle* (Fribourg, 1950), p. 26. See also Journet, *L'Eglise du Verbe incarné*, I, p. 81.

perpetuated until his return by the commemoration of his sacrifice in the Eucharist and in the dispensation of the new sacraments, which are destined to bring to each individual soul his life-giving touch through space and time.

Christ, as king and prophet, imparts to the world the fulness of truth, and the presence of his prophetic kingship, revealed once and for all, is to be spread to the farthest confines of space and time.

We can now read, without mutilating the meaning, the words at the close of the Gospel of Saint Matthew, in which Christ himself informs us how he intends to prolong the exercise of his prophetic kingship and his priesthood by means of his disciples:

> All authority in heaven and on earth, he said, has been given to me; you, therefore, must go out, making disciples of all nations, and baptizing them in the name of the Father, and of the Son, and of the Holy Ghost, teaching them to observe all the commandments which I have given you. And behold I am with you all through the days that are coming, until the consummation of the world (Matt., XXVIII, 18-20).

It is Christ himself, endowed with all authority, who will henceforth teach by means of his disciples and who will baptize by means of them.

Jesus himself had forgiven sins, and the disciples will have to forgive sins in their turn; but it is Jesus who will forgive sins through them:

> I came upon an errand from my Father, and now I am sending you out in my turn. With that, he breathed on them, and said to them, Receive the Holy Spirit; when you forgive men's sins, they are forgiven, when you hold them bound, they are held bound (John, XX, 21-23).

In the same way, Jesus himself explained the Scriptures
to his disciples on the road to Emmaus; and Philip in his
turn will have to explain them to the Ethiopian (see
Acts, VIII, 31ff.); but it is Jesus who will explain the
Scriptures through him.

5. THE PERPETUATION OF THE SANCTITY OF CHRIST

The priesthood and kingship of Christ are designed to
communicate the holiness of Christ to the world. This is
the supreme consideration. The perpetuation of the
priesthood and the kingship of Christ is likewise intended for the perpetuation of this sanctity of Christ in
the Church, which is his Body.

Here again between Head and Body there is a difference in level which is insurmountable. The sanctity of
Christ is unique and belongs to the hypostatic order; the
sanctity of the Church belongs to the order of created
grace and the indwelling of the Holy Spirit:

> If a man has any love for me, he will be true to my word;
> and then he will win my Father's love, and we will both
> come to him, and make our continual abode with him.
> (John, XIV, 23). Do you not understand that you are
> God's temple, and that God's Spirit has his dwelling in
> you? (I Cor., III, 16). The love of God has been poured
> out in our hearts by the Holy Spirit, whom we have re-
> ceived (Rom., V, 5).

But here again the difference in level does not destroy
the homogeneity. It is Christ who lives in his Church:
". . . and yet I am alive; or rather, not I; it is Christ
that lives in me. True, I am living, here and now, this
mortal life; but my real life is the faith I have in the Son
of God, who loved me, and gave himself for me" (Gal.,

II, 20). It is the same life which passes from the vine to the branches (See John, XV, 4-5). The Church is the Spouse. It is Christ-like (*christoconforme*) and Christ-forming (*christoconformante*). The only-begotten Son is ". . . the eldest-born among many brethren," and the latter are "his heirs too" (Rom., VIII, 29 and 17). The life of Christ, eternal life, also continues to dwell in time: "Beloved, we are sons of God *even now* . . ." (I John, III, 2). "The man who eats my flesh and drinks my blood *enjoys* eternal life . . . He who eats my flesh, and drinks my blood, *lives continually* in me, and I in him" (John, VI, 55, 57).

Christianity continually appears as a pouring out of the fulness (*pleroma*) of Christ in space and time. That is its most profound definition. It is what Christ pours out on us from his superabundance. Christ finally wished that even his Mother should become our Mother:

And Jesus seeing his mother there, and the disciple, too, whom he loved, standing by, said to his mother, Woman, this is thy son. Then he said to the disciple, This is thy mother. And from that hour the disciple took her into his own keeping (John, XIX, 26-27).

4

THE MNEMIC CONCEPT OF CHRISTIANITY

According to this concept, the beginning of Christianity was marked by a unique event, a *hapax*, which will allegedly be rediscovered much later in all its purity, quite apart from any kind of historical continuity, thanks to an analysis of texts which will then be regarded as scientific, but which will be subject to constant revision. Christianity is the recollection of an original Gospel event, attained by a method of interpretation which will result in the creation, in turn, of a new living tradition (this can hardly be denied) among those who accept this method.

These are briefly some of the conclusions which those who hold this concept have reached.

1. THE SUPPER HAS ONLY A SYMBOLICAL MEANING

Christ is the Word made flesh, who appeared among us. He has returned to heaven and left us a simple memorial

of his earthly sojourn in the Eucharist. Whatever bene-
ficial effect his bodily presence once had, it could not
be of any further benefit to us now: "the flesh is of no
avail." We must be content with the mere historical
memory of his appearance in the flesh long ago.

"By a single offering he has completed his work, for
all time, in those whom he sanctifies" (Heb., X, 14).
He died in order to redeem the world. There is now no
longer any real continuity between him and us, who are
his members. There is no need for us to share in his offering and redemptive sacrifice in the way in which the
body is united with the head, for the purpose of making
our offering with him and redeeming the world with
him. Everything depends upon a past event which does
not extend into the present and which only needs to be
kept alive as something to be remembered.

2. THE SACRAMENTS ARE MERE SIGNS

Christ does not continue to have contact with individual
souls and to inspire them with special, Christ-forming
graces by means of the sacraments, as he did when he
was on earth. He is content to leave behind him sacraments which are mere signs, whose sole purpose is to
recall the fact that he once saved the world and to invite
us to join together in the recollection of this past event.

3. THE TEXT OF SCRIPTURE IS THE SOLE RULE OF FAITH

Christ definitely does not continue to teach the truth
infallibly. His revelation has been noted down in Holy
Scripture. It was rediscovered after the lapse of fifteen
centuries with the help of methods of exegesis available

at that time. Hence a new form of Christianity arose, a Christianity of the Scriptures, which no longer has any need of being explained orally or infallibly, as on the road to Emmaus (See Luke XXIV, 13ff.), or on the other road which goes from Jerusalem to Gaza and the desert (See Acts, VIII, 26ff.). Since then, by a sort of fatal process, this new interpretation of the Scriptures has assumed the rigid form of a tradition. Scripture and the Catholic Church are often contrasted with one another, when in reality it is two traditional ways of interpreting Scripture which are being opposed to one another, the new and the old.

4. IMPUTED GRACE AND JUSTIFICATION BY FAITH ALONE

Christ no longer pours out the ontological superabundance of his grace and truth on the Church which ". . . in all its beauty, no stain, no wrinkle, no such disfigurement . . . holy . . . spotless" (Eph., V, 27) is called upon to continue saving the world through him, with him, and in him. Divine grace has become a pardon granted by God externally to those beings whom he decides to declare just, while they remain basically and fatally sinners, *simul peccatores et justi.*

Christianity has become the unbroken continuity of faith, the firm belief of those who in spite of their sin regard themselves as justified (Luther), or predestined (Calvin).

Christians, including the Virgin herself at the foot of the Cross, are powerless to become co-redemptive members of the ". . . one mediator between God and men, Jesus Christ, who is a man, like them, and gave himself as a ransom for them all" (I Tim., II, 5-6).

5. CATHOLICITY OR DISCONTINUITY

Let there be no misunderstanding. We do not deny the necessity for anyone who believes in the Catholic faith to have constant recourse to the sources, above all, to the scriptural sources. We are simply distinguishing between two methods of having recourse to the sources. The one holds fast to the main stream of the current which gave birth to the scriptural sources themselves at a unique and special moment, and thereafter continues to proceed on its way and to exist by means of them until the end of time. The other, rejecting the notion of divine catholicity in time, attempts to regain the scriptural sources in one leap.

I only attempt to point out here some of the principal views to which the mnemic concept of Christianity has led. Other characteristics could be mentioned, but it must be repeated that these views do not always form an inseparable whole in actual practice. They can be separated from each other and even held along with views which depend on the concept I have called ontological. This is true with regard to certain forms of Protestantism.

Finally, it is evident that these views, which from the Catholic point of view are regarded as serious alterations of Christianity, can be professed, because of invincible ignorance, even by those who hold enlightened views on other points. If these persons live in divine charity, and in the last resort this is the secret of God himself, they belong to the one true Church, to the one true form of Christianity, in a way that is only a beginning and still full of obstacles, but which is already saving, in spite of their erroneous notions about the Church.

6. DOUBTS ABOUT THE INFALLIBILITY OF THE SCRIPTURES

After a period of confidence and boldness the new interpretation of Christianity, by reason of the difficulties
to which it had given rise, has opened the door to a
period of discouragement. In the Church of England,
for example, quite a few of the leading lights today hold
that Christianity can be reduced to the simple fact of
the ineffable manifestation of God in Christ. Whatever
serves to hand on this transcendent fact, whether it be
formulation by ecumenical councils or the formulation
of the New Testament itself, is to be treated with the
greatest respect and cannot be lightly disregarded, but
still cannot be regarded as infallible. In a completely
different way Karl Barth arrives at similar conclusions:
the Bible is not in itself the word of God, but something
human, mundane, and fallible, the written witness of
the events by which God intervened and spoke, and the
place where there is the most likely chance that he is
speaking to us *hic et nunc.*

It is curious to note that in his day Saint Irenaeus was
obliged to answer not only those who relied upon Scripture as opposed to tradition, but also those who in the
name of a more secret tradition cast doubt on the truth
of Scripture under the pretext that the apostles and
Jesus himself had spoken to men through it in accordance with their prejudices:

> If the apostles adapted their words to the ideas which
> men had formerly held, no one received the truth from
> them: moreover, no one received it from the Lord, for
> the Gnostics maintain that the Lord himself spoke in that
> way. Thus the apostles themselves did not know the
> truth, but in accordance with the particular notion they

had of God received a doctrine suited to their understanding. In accordance with this reasoning the norm of
truth does not lie with anyone. . . . The Coming of the
Lord will appear superfluous and without point, if he
came to approve and preserve the notion which each one
previously had of God.[1]

---

[1] St. Irenaeus, *Adversus haereses*, III, 12, 6. Cf. *Ibid.*, 5, 2.

5

CATHOLICISM AND PROTESTANTISM

I shall continue to ignore those Protestants who no longer believe that Jesus is the Word made flesh, at the same time true God and true Man. Only that portion of Protestantism which still believes in the divinity of Christ will concern us here.

When Catholics search for the reason—perhaps not the most fundamental reason, but certainly the most apparent one—which lies at the basis of all the differences between Catholicism and Protestantism, they always arrive at conclusions similar to those which we have just outlined, without having to agree beforehand on what their attitude will be.

1. VIEWS OF FATHER HENRI DE LUBAC ON THE CHURCH, THE EUCHARIST, TRADITION, THE TEACHING OFFICE

This is the way, for example, in which Father de Lubac, considering the close connection which always exists

between Eucharistic doctrine and doctrine about the
Church, compares Catholicism and Protestantism:

> Realism in the Eucharist and realism in the Church; these
> two realisms depend on each other and guarantee each
> other. Realism in the Church entails realism in the Eucha-
> rist, and the latter in turn confirms the former. The same
> unity of the Word is reflected in the one and in the other.
> Today it is above all our faith in the real presence, made
> more explicit thanks to generations of controversy and
> analysis, which assists us to believe in the Church as a
> body. The mystery of the Church, effectively typified by
> the mystery of the altar, must have the same nature and
> the same profundity. In the ancient world the point of
> view was often the reverse. They tended to emphasize the
> effect, rather than the cause. But the realism of their
> views about the Church, which are everywhere clearly
> and explicitly stated, assures us at the same time and to
> the same extent of the realism of their views about the
> Eucharist, whenever there is any need for this. For the
> cause must be adequate to its effect.

By virtue of the same inner logic—those who in modern
times attempt to explain away the traditional notion of the
Church as the body of Christ also find that they must
explain away the reality of Christ's presence in the Eucharist. Hence Calvin is obliged to maintain that there is the
same kind of virtual presence of Christ in the sacrament
as there is among the faithful. His reason is the same in
both cases: "For he is in heaven and we are here on
earth." Moreover, when the Calvinist pastor Claude
wishes to deny the evidence drawn from the Fathers
which Catholic apologists cite in favor of the Catholic
doctrine of the Eucharist, he finds he is obliged to question the meaning of their passages concerning the Church.
Indeed, how could the Church really be built in the first
place, how could the members all be gathered in an organization which is really one, by means of a sacrament
which only symbolically contains him whose body it is to

become and who alone can make it one? Saint Augustine himself becomes meaningless and all his suggestive mysticism vanishes in empty formulas, if in analyzing the implications of his doctrine we refuse to recognize there the faith of the common tradition. For him the Eucharist is much more than a symbol, it is truly the sacrament *quo in hoc tempore consociatur Ecclesia*, since the water and wine of the sacrifice, like the water and wine which ran from the Cross, are themselves the sacraments *quibus aedificatur Ecclesia*. The presence is real because it realizes.[1]

It could likewise be shown that the doctrine of imputed justice necessarily entails a doctrine of the Church emptied of its ontological meaning.

The same theologian, in a recent study which is a brilliant profession of faith, speaks of the man who wishes to be fully Christian: "The Church has taken possession of his heart." It spares him the "doubts and disappointments of Churches made by man." Such a man

believes, both that God revealed all things once and for all in his Son, and that divine wisdom at the same time adapts our understanding to the mystery of Christ in each age, in and through the Church. He knows perfectly well that in the exercise of its teaching office the Church not only does not teach any new doctrine, it says nothing of its own. . . . Scripture, Tradition, Teaching Office: these three things he considers as the threefold, unique channel by which the word of God reaches him. He considers them, not as infringing upon or limiting the sphere of each other, but rather as depending upon each other, as contributing to each other, confirming, clarifying and magnifying each other. He realizes that their fate is bound

[1] Henri de Lubac, S.J., *Corpus mysticum, L'Eucharistie et l'Eglise au moyen âge* (Paris, 1944), pp. 288-290.

together. He sees in this a *funiculus triplex* which cannot be broken.

It is the Church which daily teaches us the law of Jesus Christ, puts into our hands his Gospel, and assists us to interpret it.

What would have been the fate of this small book, or in what condition would it have come down to us, if in some impossible way it had not been edited, preserved, and commented upon generally by Catholic Christianity at large? What corruptions and mutilations would it not have undergone in its text and in its meaning? But why dwell on these imaginary possibilities? History itself is sufficiently eloquent in this regard. The doctrinal errors which appeal to the Gospel for authority are legion.[2]

2. VIEWS OF FATHER YVES CONGAR ON THE RELATION OF HOLY SCRIPTURE AND TRADITION

Father Congar has criticized the Protestant position with a great deal of acumen. Speaking of the living deposit of faith, the *paradosis*, which Christ left to the primitive Church and to the apostles, and of its written expression in the inspired books of Scripture, he reminds us that philological and exegetical study of this written expression can prove most fruitful in directing our attention to certain important aspects of the revealed deposit of faith, but it is wholly inadequate to enable us to attain that deposit itself.

The Church does not derive the contents of its faith, properly speaking, from Scripture; it discovers it there, something which is quite different. The contents of faith are embodied in tradition, *i quod traditum est.* . . .

[2] Henri de Lubac, S.J., "L'Eglise notre mère," *Etudes* (Jan., 1953).

There is more to be found in the reality itself than in anything which is said about it.

When we are told, for example, that *kecharitomene* in Luke, I, 28, means favored, not full of grace, and therefore cannot serve as the basis for Catholic theological doctrine about the Blessed Virgin, my answer is that philology is an excellent thing and that the science of exegesis based upon philology, archaeology and history, is necessary and good; but they cannot determine God's revelation, which has been handed on to the Church and to which the Bible bears witness. The only power sufficiently trustworthy and intelligent to interpret the gift of God is not the mind of the exegete, but the mind of the Church, formed in it by the Holy Spirit. I have respect for, and frequently consult, the science of the exegetes, but I refuse to accept their teaching office.[3]

Father Congar refers to A. Nygren, who, in studying the notion of *agape* (charity) in Scripture, thought that he could conclude that

the idea of a return to God and of a love which assists men to return to him could not be a Christian notion. This is not the place to show how such a view can only be held if Holy Scripture itself is expurgated. . . . What I wish to note here in connection with my argument is the fundamental error which consists in believing that we can determine what Christians ought to believe by an exegetical-historical study of the notion of *agape*. What Christians ought to believe is *id quod traditum est, id quod traditur,* that is, the reality of Christianity itself; this has always been based upon the love of God and drawing near to him in love, in Saint Paul's case too. With regard to this reality all the exegesis of Nygren can do . . . is to draw our attention to certain important aspects

[3] Yves Congar, O.P., *Vraie et fausse réforme dans l'Eglise* (Paris, 1950), p. 498.

which are part of the tradition of the Church and which
can be shown to be such from the most important monument of this tradition, Holy Scripture.

I would say the same of the notion of Church . . .
Ekklesia means assembly, gathering. . . . The word
Ekklesia, from the philological point of view, means just
that; exegetically however, in the light of usage and various meanings in the Bible, it means more; recent studies
in this connection have shown that this is so, and have
revealed aspects of the word which were unknown to the
Reformers. But above all the reality designated by this
word . . . far surpasses the realm of the dictionary. The
Church has not been given to us in a definition, or in a
text, as if the Bible were a mere collection of paradigms
in accordance with which men were henceforth to con-
struct the edifice of Christianity; it has been given to us,
and then further handed on to us, in its reality, a reality
which in its formative stages has been illustrated for us
in an important and decisive way in Holy Scripture, but
which surpasses this evidence and cannot be tied down to
the written word,[4]

as interpreted according to the principles of philology.

The things which one is most likely to misunderstand, if
one admits the rule of the Bible, are the most hidden, and
in many respects the most profound, aspects of the Christian reality; for example, obedience, chastity, poverty, the
role of the Blessed Virgin, and the life of the sacraments.[5]

3. A MISUNDERSTANDING OF THE MYSTERY OF THE INCAR-
NATION LIES AT THE ROOT OF PROTESTANTISM

Father Congar mentions certain reasons for the Protestant misinterpretation of Christianity which are even

[4] Congar, *op. cit.,* p. 500.
[5] *Ibid.,* p. 501.

more significant. He finds that a misunderstanding of the doctrine of the Incarnation lies at the root of things:

> Once again we find that there is a parallel between the theology of the Church and that of justification; in both cases, in order that everything may come from Jesus Christ, they wish everything to remain in Jesus Christ; they place along side and superimpose on the sinful and unbelieving nature of man that which is purely spiritual, a pure act of God. The Church does not live on what it is, but on what God is for it in Jesus Christ; this kind of speculation results in a concept of a world which is purely divine, touching, but still outside, another world which is purely human. There can no longer be any question of a Church in the traditional Western or Eastern sense.

A defective Christology, it seems to me, lies at the root of this trouble. They retain the essential wording of the doctrine defined at Ephesus and Chalcedon; the Reformers did the same, and so does Karl Barth today. But do they understand by the traditional formulas all that Catholic teaching sees in them? We may question whether they do, when we find Luther insisting on a presence in, under, and with, a mere concomitance, in the case of the Incarnation as well as the Eucharist and the Church; or when we find Zwingli specifying that our faith in Christ should be addressed only to his divinity; or when Calvin bends over backward to avoid using the word *Theotokos;* or finally, when Karl Barth speaks of the Incarnation in such a way that it is made to seem less like an entry of God into our world, a gift that God makes of his Son to the world, than as an act of the Word of God coming to announce the condemnation of sin and pardon in Christ, who is condemned to death and raised from the dead. Of course, we must not exaggerate. There is one fundamental fact on which, thanks to the grace of God, we may found our hopes for unity; we believe, both sides, in Jesus Christ, the Son of God who was made Man. I merely mention here the fact, which has an undeniable impor-

tance, that the great Protestant dogmatic theologians tend
to explain away the immanent realism inherent in the
doctrine of the Incarnation in favor of a doctrine which
implies less union between God and his creature man.[6]

We may recall here the words in which John Adam
Möhler summed up his impression of Luther: "What
the words, 'the Word was made flesh, became man,'
mean was never clear to Luther." The misunderstanding of the instrumental causality involved in the sacraments is fatally bound up with the misunderstanding
of the higher instrumental causality involved in the
humanity of Christ, and finally with a misunderstanding
of the mystery of the hypostatic union. In a recent work
Father Congar gives a penetrating analysis of the Chris-
tological views of the Reformers, and especially of
Luther:

> Luther is not interested in the metaphysical aspect of
> Christology, but rather in its dramatic aspects. It makes
> little difference to him whether Christ has two natures
> according to the formula, so to speak, of his inner nature;
> what interests him is that God came in the person of
> Christ for the purpose of taking our sins away in him, and
> giving us his justice. That is why Luther has a concept
> of the communication of properties or idioms which
> differs from that of Christian tradition. . . . Thus we re-
> turn to our central problem, the role which humanity,
> including that of Christ, plays or does not play in the
> economy of salvation. . . . Luther sees a parallel be-
> tween and assimilates these three things: justification, the
> kingdom of God, and creation; he writes with regard to
> them that they are the works of God alone without any
> help from the humanity of Christ. The passage which
> expresses ideas of this sort reveals to us the very

[6] Congar, *op. cit.*, p. 452.

heart of Luther's thought and the difference which separates the Reformation from Catholic tradition. What Luther wants is that everything in salvation should come from God alone and be the work of God alone. . . . But this point of view is not without influence on the concept he forms of the role of Christ's humanity in the economy of salvation. It likewise can have no effect.[7]

We now see that it is the faith of Chalcedon itself which is finally being questioned. Instead of distinguishing two natures in Christ, the divine and the human, and uniting them in the unique person of the Word by means of a subordination, a penetration, an incarnation, in which the latter is illumined by the former, they tend simply to consider the two natures side by side, the human nature of Christ becoming henceforth not an instrumental cause, an "organon," but simply an occasion of our salvation, a mere phenomenal shell, in which the invisible God made his appearance, who as such is alone the Savior of men.

This is one of the passages of Luther, cited by Father Congar, to which Protestants constantly refer:

Christ has two natures. What is the meaning of that to me? If he bears the marvelous and consoling name of Christ, it is because of the ministry and the blemish which he took upon himself; that is what gives him his name. That he is by nature man and God is of concern only to him. But the fact that he has devoted his ministry and poured out his love to become my savior and my redeemer is particularly comforting and consoling to me. . . . To believe in Christ does not mean that Christ is a person who is both man and God, that has no meaning for anybody; it means that this person is Christ, that is to

[7] Yves Congar, O.P., *Le Christ, Marie et l'Eglise* (Paris, 1952), pp. 34-37. Father Congar is right in attempting to concentrate "ecumenical discussion" on the definition of Chalcedon.

say, that for our sakes he came out from God and came into the world; his name derives from this function.[8]

What sophism is concealed by these pious words? According to Catholic teaching God gave us his Son twice: once at Christmas in the mystery of the Incarnation with his two natures united in one divine person; and once on Good Friday in the mystery of Redemption and infinite compensation which he paid on the Cross for the sins of the world. Jesus saved us by being what he was, before saving us by doing what he did. The mystery of the Incarnation and the mystery of Redemption are only two moments corresponding to the being and action of one unique mystery, the mystery of the redemptive Incarnation. The second moment is contained in the first and the first in the second. The action of Christ flows from the being of Christ. The being of Christ exists for the sake of his action, not like a means for an end, but like a spring with respect to its overflowing. The Incarnation is related to the Redemption in the same way that fulness is to superabundance. Christ dies for us, not in order to disappear before us, but in order to make us into his crown: "All those who from the first were known to him, he has destined from the first to be moulded into the image of his Son, who is thus to become the eldest-born among many brethren" (Rom., VIII, 29). What Christ is for me depends essentially on what Christ is for himself. What Christ is for himself is of more importance to God and to the kingdom of God than what Christ is to me. That is the important thing in Christianity: "He alone triumphs over the world, who believes that Jesus *is* the

[8] Congar, *Le Christ, Marie et l'Eglise,* p. 33.

Son of God" (I John, V, 5). Luther maintains the faith
of Chalcedon, that there are two natures in Christ, the
divine and the human, existing in the one person of
the Son of God; but secret reasons compel him to shift
the emphasis in a way that will turn out to be disastrous.
He never clearly understood what is meant by the Word
being made flesh. Möhler was right.

In order to clarify the mystery of the Incarnation, let
us reflect on the way in which man's soul is joined to his
body. Is man a beast in which an angel dwells? Do his
corporal and spiritual natures exist in him side by side
in a sort of juxtaposition? Is the former only the occasion for the existence of the latter? Or, on the contrary,
is not his corporal nature subordinate to his spiritual
nature? Is it essentially illuminated, elevated, informed,
and transformed by it? Is it in relation to the soul truly
an instrumental cause and "organon"? If we think of the
relation between the human and divine nature of Christ
in this way, as the Fathers always did, making allow-
ance of course for the profound changes which are necessary in passing from the order of nature to the order
of revelation, have we not grasped the meaning of the
faith of Chalcedon? How could anyone maintain, when
we distinguish two natures in Christ, the divine and
the human, and hold that they are joined together by an
ontological and vital subordination of the second to the
first, that there is any Monophysitism, or confusion of
the two natures, involved in this? Monophysitism denies
the distinction of the two natures in Christ, the divine
and the human. Nestorianism denies the uniqueness in
Christ of the divine person which unites in itself the two
natures, divine and human, by vitally subordinating the
latter to the former. "But Jesus said, Somebody touched

me; I can tell that power has gone out from me" (Luke, VIII, 46).

4. THE ULTIMATE REASON FOR THE DIFFERENCES BETWEEN CATHOLICISM AND PROTESTANTISM

If we look for the ultimate reason for the differences between Catholicism—and in this respect Catholic and Orthodox teaching are the same—and Protestantism, we are soon inclined to point to the different forms of spirituality which they embody. On the one hand there is the spirituality of the Incarnation, or in a broader sense the spirituality of the transfiguration of matter by the spirit. This is the Catholic form of spirituality with its doctrine of the Incarnation, the instrumental causality of the sacraments of the New Law, the visibility of the Church, the resurrection of the flesh, the immediate creation of visible things by God himself, etc. On the other hand we have a sort of spirituality of disincarnation, or in a broader sense a spirituality of the separation of matter and spirit. That is the anti-Catholic form of spirituality with its thousand forms, which tends to deny the creation of the visible world by God himself, the occurrence of miracles, the resurrection of the body, the visible Church, the instrumental causality of the sacraments of the new law, the Incarnation, etc.

On a more metaphysical plane we may see the opposition as one between a dogmatic view of the analogy of being, in accordance with which the divine privileges, especially divine sanctity, can be communicated analogically to creatures—as existence once was—without affecting adversely the divine transcendence, but rather manifesting it. On the other hand we have a dogmatic

view of the uniqueness of being, which can only safeguard the divine transcendence by denying any possibility for the divine privileges to be communicated,
especially divine sanctity: either a) to the humanity of
Christ because of the fear of Monophysitism; or b) to
creatures because of the fear of idolatry.

6

TWO CONCEPTS OF THE CHURCH
ACCORDING TO A PROTESTANT VIEW

Before leaving these general notions it might be useful to examine the way in which two contrasting views about the Church have gained currency in ecumenical circles since the conference at Amsterdam in 1948; one is the horizontal concept, which is said to be the Catholic view, and the other is the vertical concept, or the Protestant view. This is the way the two positions are stated by an Anglican theologian closely in touch with ecumenical thinking, as reported by Father Congar in his recent book:

> There are two different and irreconcilable points of view: the first considers the Church as a body existing in space and time, with an historical existence like any entity of this world, its principle of continuity being that of a real historical organism. The opposite point of view maintains that the principle of the Church's continuity is not to be

found here on earth in the categories of space and time, but belongs entirely and necessarily to the invisible world which our risen Lord Jesus Christ entered, who is the same yesterday, today and eternally, and who becomes incarnate [is it meant that Christ in glory is to be thought of as "disincarnate"?], as he wishes and when he wishes, in this or that group of human beings whom he calls to himself and who respond to this call through faith.[1]

From the Catholic point of view this passage calls for three principal remarks:

a) The distinction proposed here is not a good one. Both principles are claimed by both sides. Thus, the two continuities, one horizontal in time and the other vertical between eternity and time, are considered to be inseparable in the Catholic view of the Church. Likewise, to the extent to which Protestants since the Reformation are able to agree on a common interpretation of Scripture, does this not amount to a certain horizontal continuity in space and time, which they claim for themselves? But this last continuity is mnemic, not ontological.

b) Horizontal continuity. The Catholic Church is in time, not, as commonly alleged, "like an entity of this world," but as an entity which is in this world but not of this world. There are two ways of existing in time: that of the kingdoms of this world and that of the kingdom of Jesus which is not of this world. If this distinction is denied, what are we to think of the thirty-three years in which Jesus lived in time? Can we say that his human life was an entity of this world? In that case, we would be separating his humanity from his divinity,

---

[1] Congar, *Le Christ, Marie et l'Eglise,* p. 11. Father Congar here cites the distinction, but does not critically analyze it.

and while continuing perhaps to acknowledge the mystery of the Incarnation, we would show that we had already failed to understand it.

c) Vertical continuity. The horizontal continuity in time which Catholics claim is not exclusive, but on the contrary is essentially dependent on the vertical continuity connecting eternity with time. Hence the horizontal continuity of the waves caused by the stone which falls into the water supposes the unbroken vertical action of gravity. It is Christ himself, the same yesterday, today and eternally, who continues to pour out and maintain grace in his Church, who himself teaches and baptizes by means of those whom he assists to teach and baptize. He acts upon his Church and upon each individual soul; if it is without the assistance of his ministers, the subject is affected immediately or there is said to be an immediation of the subject; if he acts by means of his ministers, the subject is affected through them or there is a mediation of the subject. In both cases, he is the one who acts upon the Church and each soul as he wishes; he is the one on whom the weight of the whole edifice rests continually and at every moment; there is always an immediation of power and virtue from him to the Church. According to the Protestant concept, on the other hand, in which the sacraments become mere signs, in which justice is merely imputed, in which faith is the firm belief that one is justified or predestined, what becomes of this vertical action of Christ on the Church and the soul? Vertical continuity, like horizontal continuity, is reduced to mere devotion to the signs which God affords us—he gives us only signs—this continuity is no longer ontological, merely mnemic.

7

IS THERE A PERMANENT AND INFALLIBLE
TEACHING OFFICE IN THE CHURCH?

God was moved by love to impart to men the fulness of
his revelation through Christ and the apostles; was he
also moved by love to guarantee the infallible teaching
of this revelation until the end of time? Or did he leave
men after the death of the apostles with a mute text
which each could interpret as he saw fit? This is the
first and most general question we intend to ask in considering Prof. Cullmann's book.

1. THE MISSION OF THE APOSTLES TO ALL NATIONS UNTIL
    THE END OF THE WORLD, ACCORDING TO MATTHEW AND
    JOHN

Christ is the Redeemer for all time. "By a single offering he has completed his work, for all time, in those
whom he sanctifies" (Heb., X, 14). Moreover, he

knows the extent of the time which he is redeeming. "What Jesus Christ was yesterday, and is today, he remains for ever" (Heb., XIII, 8). The Gospel has too many passages in which he declares that there is nothing hidden between the Father and himself for anyone to doubt that he knew the exact time of his return, his second coming (*Parousia*). When he tells the disciples that no one knows the day or the hour of the end of the world, ". . . they are known to nobody . . . not even to the Son; only the Father knows them," (Mark, XIII, 32) the only possible explanation of the passage is that he does not know the exact time as something which he can reveal to them, as he explicitly states in the Acts of the Apostles, I, 7: "It is not for you to know the times and seasons which the Father has fixed by his own authority."

When Christ sends the Eleven out into the world, he reminds them solemnly that he is the Master of time: "All authority in heaven and on earth, he said, has been given to me; you, therefore, must go out, making disciples of all nations . . . And behold I am with you all through the days that are coming, until the consummation of the world" (Matt., XXVIII, 18-20). The Eleven cannot go in person to all nations in space and to all generations in time. It is by means of the missionary work which they actually begin, and by means of the actual sound of their preaching, which will radiate from Pentecost like a succession of waves until the end of time, that they will reach all nations and all generations. This is the real missionary work and the actual preaching of the word which will be assisted by Christ all through the days until the consummation of the world.

The same Love which infallibly brought us the truth will infallibly guard it to the end.

In the great prayer offered up shortly before his death, in which he asks that the work of the Father which he is about to accomplish shall be perpetuated until the end of time in those who will be one in him through faith and love, the Savior thinks first of all of his apostles: "Thou hast sent me into the world on thy errand, and I have sent them into the world on my errand" (John, XVII, 18); then he turns his thoughts to those who will believe through their word: "It is not only for them that I pray; I pray for those *who are to find faith in me through their word;* that they may all be one; that they too may be one in us, as thou Father, art in me, and I in thee . . ." (John, XVII, 20-21). This prayer, which the Father cannot help but hear, asks for —and obtains—unity in the knowledge of faith and love until the end of time: "I have revealed, and will reveal, thy name to them; so that the love thou hast bestowed upon me may dwell in them, and I, too, may dwell in them" (John, XVII, 26). Thus there will be disciples, who, through the word of the apostles, will believe in Jesus and who, being one in the knowledge of the Father, will be one in love.[1] This will be so forever. If the world is to go on existing after the personal death of the apostles, their word will at least continue to prolong the infallible word of Jesus, and their missionary work will continue to bring about unity in the knowledge of the Father and in love.

This explanation of Matthew, XXVIII, 18-20, and of John, XVII, 20-26, is crystal-clear. It does not force the

[1] On the full meaning of the prayer of Jesus for unity, see Journet, *L'Eglise du Verbe incarné,* II, pp. 1289-1297.

44

meaning of the texts. It simply reminds us of the fact that the one who is speaking is Jesus. This is the point of view taken by the Vatican Council at the beginning of its *Dogmatic Constitution on the Church of Christ:*

> The eternal Pastor and Bishop of our souls (I Peter, II, 25), in order to perpetuate the salutary work of Redemption, decreed the foundation of Holy Church, in which all the faithful should be gathered together as in the house of the living God by the bond of the same faith and the same charity. That is why, before his glorification, he prayed to his Father not only for the apostles, but also for those who would believe in him through their word, in order that they might be one, as the Son himself and the Father are one (John, XVII, 20). And that is why, after choosing apostles for himself from the world, he sent them as he himself had been sent by the Father (John, XX, 21), thus indicating his wish that there should be pastors and teachers in his Church until the consummation of the world (Matt., XXVIII, 20).[2]

2. OMISSION OF A PASSAGE FROM MATTHEW BY PROF. CULLMANN: THE SUPPOSED IGNORANCE OF JESUS

This is not the way in which Prof. Cullmann interprets these passages.

To be sure, he vigorously rejects interpretations like that of Albert Schweitzer, which represent Jesus as believing that the Kingdom of God would be realized at the moment of his death. He has little difficulty in showing that Jesus contemplates a mission of the apostles among the Gentiles before the end comes:

> For Jesus his own death undoubtedly constitutes the central event in the redemptive process that leads to the

[2] Denzinger, No. 1821. See pages 70 and 105.

Kingdom of God. But he sees the tension between the present and the future; it is already present in his lifetime, and he knows that by his death it is not yet removed.[3]

Prof. Cullmann even goes so far as to admit with Catholics, in a certain sense, that the Kingdom of God is anticipated in history:

> Even in Jesus' own preaching the Kingdom of God is on the one hand still not present, for it comes only at the end; and yet in the presence of Jesus it has already broken in: "If I cast out demons by the Spirit of God, then the Kingdom of God has already come to you" (Matt., XII, 28). . . . Thus there can be no doubt that Jesus himself reckons with such an anticipation of the Kingdom of God; in him the decision has already occurred, even if the completion is expected only in the final time. . . . There does exist on this point a certain difference between Jesus and the Primitive Church; Jesus is conscious that the fulfilment is present *in his person,* while the Primitive Church sees the fulfilment *in the Church.* But there is no conflict here at all. Rather, the fulfilment in the person of Jesus leads directly to the fulfilment in the Church, and the fulfilment in the Church points back in turn to the fulfilment in the person of Jesus. . . . A direct contradiction between the future Kingdom of God and the already realized people of God is only a construction built on the basis of modern thinking. . . .[4]

Prof. Cullmann insists on these notions, which are far from being those of all Protestants:

> The idea of the continuation of the work of Christ in the visible earthly Church I affirm, since I find it especially in the Gospel of John as a central declaration. Therefore, as far as I am concerned—I do not speak here at all in

[3] Cullmann, *Peter, Disciple, Apostle, Martyr,* p. 200.
[4] *Ibid.,* pp. 194-195.

the name of official "Protestant theology"—it is not true
that on this point the common basis for discussion is lack-
ing. It should be sufficiently clear from my previous writings that I really take seriously the fact that the present
in which we stand, the period of the Church, belongs in
the redemptive history; this history, to be sure, must continually find its norm in the apostolic period of revelation as the central point of time.[5]

Yet, in spite of many important views which he shares
with Catholics on the precise point which we are now
discussing, the permanence of an infallible teaching
office, Prof. Cullmann does not succeed in freeing himself from the circle of Protestant thinking. This is evident from the way in which he interprets the two passages from the Gospels of Matthew and John which we
have just studied.

We must mention first of all a remark which he makes
in passing, but which nevertheless causes us to have serious misgivings:

> To be sure, Jesus scarcely reckons with a duration of
> millenniums, but he does assume that there will be a
> rather brief period of time between his resurrection and
> return.[6]

Thus we see that Jesus can no longer be the one to
whom we pray. He has ceased to be the one who said
to Pascal: "I thought of thee in my agony, such drops
of blood I shed for thee." [7]

It follows from this—at least this is the obvious
conclusion I draw from these remarks—that the great

[5] Cullmann, *op. cit.*, p. 235.
[6] *Ibid.*, p. 201.
[7] Blaise Pascal, *Pensées,* translated C. K. Paul (London: Bohn Library,
1895), p. 232.

promise which appears at the end of the Gospel of
Saint Matthew: "All authority in heaven and on earth
. . . has been given to me; you, therefore, must go out,
making disciples of all nations . . . And behold I am
with you all through the days that are coming, until the
consummation of the world," is emptied of all meaning
and effect. Christ is not even the person he considered
himself to be, the one to whom all authority is said to
have been given over the time which elapses from
Pentecost to the second coming (*Parousia*). He is no
longer in a position to promise his infallible and continuing assistance to those whom he sends towards a
future which he is no longer to dominate and which is
destined to remain unknown to him. In fact, Prof. Cullmann attaches no particular importance to this passage
of Saint Matthew, which in our opinion is of the utmost
importance. He does not deny its genuineness; he simply
omits discussion of it.

3. INTERPRETATION OF THE PASSAGE IN JOHN: THE UNITY
OF THE CHURCH FOUNDED MERELY ON THE WRITINGS OF
THE APOSTLES

In his opinion, the passage which presents the priestly
prayer of Jesus is the ". . . only New Testament text
that explicitly speaks of the relation of the apostles to
the Church that follows them." [8] How does he interpret
it? We must recall the context. Jesus has just prayed to
the Father on behalf of the apostles: "Thou hast sent
me into the world on thy errand, and I have sent them
into the world on my errand." Then he adds: "It is not
only for them that I pray; I pray for those who are to

[8] Cullmann, *op. cit.*, p. 221.

48

find faith in me through their word; that they may all
be one." The ultimate desire of this mighty prayer is that
there shall be unity in the knowledge of faith and in
love (John, XVII, 18, 20, 26). Now this is the way
Prof. Cullmann looks at it: The apostles are going to die.
The mission of the apostles and the apostolic message
will cease with them. The only thing that will remain
will be what they or their disciples commit to writing.
The words, "those who find faith in me through their
word," are intended by Jesus to mean, "those who find
faith in me through their writings." The teaching of the
apostles was very soon committed to writing, those writings which have been preserved for us. We are redis-
covering the meaning of these writings today. They are
the only rule of faith for the Church. The apostles have
left a unique statement of their work, which

> continues to exist in our present as a concrete gift from
> the time of revelation. This unique gift, which constitutes
> the continuance of the apostles in the period of the
> Church, is the Apostolic Scripture. . . . Here in these
> writings we today, in the midst of the twentieth century,
> meet the person of the apostles, the person of the first
> among the apostles, Peter; in this way they continue to
> support, he continues to support, the structure of the
> Church.[9]

But these writings are capable of being interpreted
in various ways. When we happen to be confronted by
interpretations which are apparently contradictory, the
last word lies with the results of historical research. This
is the final visible foundation Christ wished to give to
the mystical unity of knowledge which he requested
for his Church before his death.

[9] Cullmann, *op. cit.*, p. 221.

Let us now re-read the words of Jesus in their context, first according to the Catholic view, and then according to the other view. We can then make our choice.[10]

[10] On the relation between the deposit of revealed truth and the teaching office of the Church and on the three meanings of the word tradition, see: "Dépot divinement révélé et magistère divinement assisté," in *Nova et Vetera*, 1950, pp. 292-301.

8

WHAT IS UNIQUE ABOUT THE MISSION OF THE
APOSTLES? IN WHAT SENSE IS THEIR
MISSION PERMANENT?

1. A FALSE DILEMMA OF PROF. CULLMANN: APOSTOLIC
   GRACE MUST EITHER PERISH WITH THE APOSTLES, OR
   SURVIVE THEM IN ITS ENTIRETY

Interpreting the words of Jesus, "those who find faith
in me through their word," to mean, "those who find
faith in me through their writings," and assuring us that
the apostles live on in the period of the Church only in
their writings, which we have only to call to mind, Prof.
Cullmann writes: "It is not confessional prejudice, but
simply the primitive Christian apostolic concept, that
leads me to affirm this." [1]

Let us pause here for a moment. Prof. Cullmann is
persuaded that the permanence of an infallible teaching
office, destined to watch over the apostolic deposit of
faith, is a notion unknown to Jesus, who "assumes" the

[1] Cullmann, *Peter, Disciple, Apostle, Martyr*, p. 221.

imminence of the end of the world. He now goes a step further. He is convinced that the notion of an infallible teaching office, which assures the purity of the apostolic deposit of faith after the death of the apostles, was regarded by primitive Christianity as something foreign to the notion of the apostolate, irreconcilable with it, and therefore rejected by it.

At first sight this appears to be an assertion which it is rather difficult to prove. How will Prof. Cullmann go about proving it? Quite simply. He claims there is an opposition, on the one hand, between a mission of the apostles, conceived as something entirely non-transferable which was to expire with the death of the apostles and would not leave any trace other than the apostolic writings, which is said to be the concept of primitive Christianity; and, on the other hand, a mission of the apostles, conceived as something entirely transferable which is to survive as such beyond the apostles, which in substance is said to be the Catholic view. It is of course not very difficult, once this opposition has been posited, to show that the second view is unacceptable; it can probably be attributed to "an Hellenic view of time." The conclusion must inevitably be that the first view is the only correct one; it would be typical of the "Judeo-Christian view of time"; this is the Protestant view.

We can only refer to the main points of Prof. Cullmann's argument. The pertinent passages are as follows:

> Here in this quite concrete application arises the problem of the New Testament conception of time, which I have discussed elsewhere.[2] Is the period when the foundation

---

[2] Oscar Cullmann, *Christ et le temps* (Paris, 1947). (English translation, *Christ and Time* [Philadelphia: The Westminster Press, 1950].) This significant work rediscovers the importance of vital truths *and*

was laid normative for the later period, in such a way that it represents the permanent unique foundation upon which the entire later structure rests once for all? Or is it normative in the sense that what happened at the beginning is continually repeated in an analogous way during the entire period of the Church, so that the promises and commissions which Jesus gave for the period of the apostolic foundation should be handed on, *without hesitation or change,* as commissions valid for Christians who live in later years? [3] . . . Can the uniqueness and unrepeatable quality which belong to the apostolic office in the New Testament be reconciled with an extension of a specifically apostolic commission to later bishops? [4]

The Catholic view, accordingly, involves a fundamental

. . . failure to grasp the basic attitude of all New Testament thought. In opposition to Hellenism, it is characteristic of the thinking of Jesus as of all Biblical thinking that *what continues has its roots in the once-for-all unique event.* A historically unique event is the redemptive event; that is, it definitely cannot be repeated but is the *foundation* of a continuing situation whose ongoing life derives from this never-to-be-repeated event.[5] This paradox lies at the basis of Jesus' saying about the future.[6]

There is no escape from the mnemic concept of Christianity.

---

associates them with views which are entirely unacceptable. The notion of divine duration without succession, *tota simul,* is here represented as a corruption of Christianity by Hellenic thought, as early as Saint Irenaeus. We find presented here a systematic treatment like that of Nygren, for whom the notion of a love which ascends from man to God is likewise said to represent an Hellenic corruption of the Christian idea of *agape.*

[3] Italics mine.
[4] Cullmann, *Peter, Disciple, Apostle, Martyr,* pp. 155-156.
[5] The words are italicized in the original.
[6] Cullmann, *Peter, Disciple, Apostle, Martyr,* p. 211.

2. ACCORDING TO CATHOLIC DOCTRINE, ON THE OTHER HAND, THE MISSION OF THE APOSTLES COMPRISES A NON-COMMUNICABLE CHARISMA WITH REFERENCE TO THE FOUNDATION OF THE CHURCH, AND A COMMUNICABLE CHARISMA WITH REFERENCE TO ITS PRESERVATION

It scarcely needs to be said that no Catholic, however charitable, could recognize the teaching of his own Church in the construction proposed by Prof. Cullmann. This teaching is rich and balanced, and an adequate expression of it must be sought in the works of the great theologians.[7] It takes into account all the passages from Scripture. In connection with the point we are here discussing it distinguishes between a mission of the apostles which is an extraordinary non-communicable charisma relating to the *foundation* of the Church, and an ordinary communicable charisma relating to the *preservation* of the Church. Here again there is a *hapax*, a primary impulse, and concentric waves which develop from this in space and time.

The extraordinary charisma is given to the apostles with a view to founding, forming, and establishing the universal Church in the world. It involves special graces which can be grouped under three headings: a) The apostles are to be the eye-witnesses of the life and resurrection of Jesus; they will be inspired by an exceptional charity which will dispose them to seal their testimony with martyrdom; b) They will receive, especially at Pentecost, the fulness of the Christian revelation; they will give expression to this orally or in writing, in re-

[7] I have attempted to give a summary in *L'Eglise du Verbe incarné*, I, p. 157ff. and p. 463ff. In connection with another point discussed further on Prof. Cullmann is kind enough to refer to this work.

sponse to special motivation by the Holy Spirit called inspiration; their teaching will be accompanied by the performance of many miracles; c) For the purpose of ruling the universal Church they will receive immediately from Christ an executive authority, that is, an authority to undertake missions, found local churches everywhere, incorporate them in the universal Church, organize them, and establish legitimate heads over them.

With the death of the apostles these privileges will cease. Those who come after them will succeed them, not with a view to *founding* the Church, but with a view to *preserving* the Church, founded once and for all by them. The mission of founding the Church must be kept absolutely distinct from the mission of preserving infallibly the Church which has already been founded; but the latter is in the nature of a prolongation, an inevitable consequence, of the former.

3. A CATHOLIC OR DISCONTINUOUS CHURCH?

The norm of faith, according to the Catholic view, is the living *paradosis,* that is, apostolic doctrine in the sense in which it has always been understood and in which it is offered to us by an infallible teaching office.

The norm of faith, according to the Protestant view, consists only in the written texts which embody apostolic doctrine with the meaning which historical research is able to restore to them after the lapse of centuries.

According to the Catholic view the revelation which was handed on to the primitive Church by Christ and the apostles is full of a meaning which is too lofty and too divine to be preserved unchanged without divine and infallible assistance. The words of Christ are understood in a literal sense: "And behold I am with you all through the days that are coming, until the consummation of the world." Any rupture of continuity with the past would necessarily mean that some innovation, originating here on earth, was being substituted for a tradition which had been divinely handed down, and that a human meaning had been substituted for a divine meaning.

According to the Protestant view, revelation communicated by Christ and the apostles to the primitive Church and once partially fixed in written form has no need of being infallibly protected by Christ. Its meaning is a subject for controversy among men; it is up to historical research to rediscover it.

The words of Saint Paul to the Ephesians, II, 20: "Apostles and prophets are the foundation on which you were built, and the chief corner-stone of it is Jesus Christ himself," may be understood in two ways. Either they mean, "You were built on the foundation of a unique revelation, given once and for all to the world by Christ and the apostles, *the infallible transmission of which will be assured all through the days that are coming until the consummation of the world.*" This is the Catholic interpretation and the interpretation of primitive Christianity. It does not deny in any way the distinctness and uniqueness of the grace given to the apostles as founders of the Church. It alone makes possible a positive assertion of catholicity of the Body of Christ in time.

Or these words mean, "You were built on the foundation of a unique revelation given to the world once and for all by Christ and the apostles; *that portion of it which is destined to be partially fixed in writing and will be rediscovered according to the methods of historical research, will be sufficient to enlighten generations which are to come."* This is the interpretation of Prof. Cullmann. It is certainly not that of primitive Christianity, of Clement, Ignatius, Irenaeus, and Tertullian. It does not safeguard the distinctness and uniqueness of the grace given to the apostles as founders of the Church, except by misunderstanding the deep mystery of the catholicity of the Body of Christ in time.

Prof. Cullmann writes:

> Thus it is absolutely irreconcilable with the New Testament concept of apostleship when a saying on the foundation of the Church that was addressed to an apostle is simply referred to future bishops. Elders and bishops certainly do take the place of the apostles, and one may call them successors, even if this expression opens the way to misunderstandings. But in any case it must not be forgotten for a moment that they occupy a completely different position, and they must not be regarded as successors in the sense of "continuers of the apostolic function." They are successors in the chronological sense, but not in their nature. *Their function follows that of the apostles, but as a fundamentally different one.* . . . Tendencies towards a so-called "apostolic succession"—are thus actually to be found in the New Testament, but with the explicit reservation that this succession, as far as it concerns the essence of the apostolate, is not to be understood in the sense of a continuation. The apostles gave over to those men the leadership, *but not their own apostolic office.* For they knew quite well that they could not hand this on at all, since it could only be given by Jesus himself directly and *without mediation.*[8]

[8] Cullmann, *Peter, Disciple, Apostle, Martyr,* pp. 219-220.

Let there be no misunderstanding on this point. It is perfectly clear that the mission of the apostles comprised a charisma which was by its very nature nontransferable. What is denied here is that in spite of a difference in level, which no one doubts, there was an infallible homogeneity and continuity between the divinely revealed deposit of faith revealed once and for all by the apostles, on the one hand, and its actual preservation through the ages by means of a divinely assisted teaching office, on the other; between the essential structure of the Church in the never-to-be-repeated days of its foundation by the apostles and the essential structure of the Church in the course of its pilgrimage through time; or, more profoundly, between the mystery of Christ as the Head and the mystery of the Church as his Body.

4. THE NORM OF TRUTH ACCORDING TO SAINT IRENAEUS

Let us recall the words of Saint Irenaeus, which date from around 180 or 190 AD, with regard to the norm of truth revealed by the apostles and transmitted by apostolic succession:

> Thus all those who wish to behold the truth can contemplate in the entire Church the tradition of the apostles manifested in every part of the world. Moreover, we can list those whom the apostles established as bishops in the various Churches and their successors down to our own day. . . .[9]

> This is the order and this is the succession in which the tradition in the Church which has come down from the apostles and the preaching of the truth have come down

[9] St. Irenaeus, *Adversus haereses*, III, 3, 1.

to our days. Therein lies a convincing proof that the living faith is one and always the same, which has been preserved in the Church from the apostles down to our own times and has been transmitted in truth.[10]

If the apostles had left us no Scripture, would it not be necessary then to follow the order of the tradition which they transmitted to those they put in charge of the Churches? It is this very word which many barbarous peoples have embraced who believe in Christ. They possess a way of salvation which is written *without ink* or paper *by the Holy Spirit in their hearts* (II Cor., III, 3), and they preserve the ancient tradition with care. . . . Those who have believed in this faith without knowing how to read are barbarians in their language as compared with ours; but in their thoughts, their customs, their manner of living, they attain to the highest wisdom because of their faith. . . .[11]

[10] Irenaeus, *Adversus haereses*, III, 3. See pages 84 and 125.
[11] *Ibid.*, III, 4, 1 and 2.

9

THE PRIVILEGE OF PETER
ACCORDING TO THE CATHOLIC VIEW

1. THE THREE IMPORTANT PASSAGES IN THE GOSPELS

The apostolic office was essentially the same for all the
apostles; all were able to bear witness to the resurrection
of Jesus; reveal Christian truth and write inspired
canonical books; and, by virtue of their jurisdictional
power, spread the gospel, found local churches everywhere and incorporate them in the universal Church.
But Peter receives in addition a unique privilege, which
raises him at once above the level of the other apostles
with respect to this third point of jurisdictional power.

This clearly follows from the account of Jesus' appearance on the shores of the lake of Tiberias:

> Jesus said to Simon Peter, Simon, son of John, dost thou
> care for me more than these others? Yes, Lord, he told
> him, thou knowest well that I love thee. And he said to
> him, Feed my lambs. . . . Then he asked him a third

question, Simon, son of John, dost thou love me? . . .
Jesus said to him, Feed my sheep (John, XXI, 15, 17).

Thereupon the Lord immediately informed Peter of
the manner of the death whereby he would glorify God,
and the prediction had been fulfilled by the time John
wrote his Gospel (XXI, 18-19). Theologians will henceforth distinguish between the apostles as *apostles*, and
the apostles as the *sheep of Christ*, who no longer enjoy
his visible presence after the Ascension and are entrusted
by him to the care of Peter, the supreme shepherd.[1] As
far as jurisdiction is concerned, the apostles are legates
of Christ, to use an expression of Saint Paul, for the
carrying out of Christ's plan, the founding of local
churches and the incorporation of these in the universal
Church; Peter alone is the vicar of Christ and possesses
supreme jurisdictional authority.[2]

[1] "The apostles may be compared with each other in two ways: 1. *as
apostles;* in this sense they were all equal; 2. *as sheep of Christ,* no
longer able to converse with him in the flesh; in this sense Peter
alone is pastor and the other apostles have been committed to his
care." Cajetan, *De comparatione auctoritatis papae et concilii seu
Ecclesiae universalis,* written at Rome on October 12, 1511 (Edit.
Pollet), No. 23.

[2] "Peter was appointed universal *vicar* of Jesus Christ; the other
apostles served as the *legates* or *delegates* of Jesus Christ according
to the words of Saint Paul (II Cor., V, 20): 'We are Christ's am-
bassadors, then, and God appeals to you through us.' And (Eph.,
VI, 20): '. . . in making known the gospel revelation, for which I
am an ambassador in chains.' This is the meaning of the word
apostle, or one who is sent." Cajetan, *op. cit.,* No. 37. The Latin for
embassy is *legatio.*

The distinction of Cajetan will be repeated by Saint Robert Bel-
larmine, *De Romano Pontifice,* Bk. I, Chapt. 11, according to whom
the apostles "possessed the highest and broadest kind of authority,
but as *apostles* or *legates,* whereas Peter possessed it as *pastor
ordinarius.*"

Saint Thomas said that Paul was the equal of Peter "*in executione
auctoritatis, non autem in auctoritate regiminis.*" *Comm. ad Gal.,* II,
11. The apostles as such are all equal, when it comes to carrying out

We must now take up the question of jurisdictional authority.

According to Saint Luke, XXII, 31-32, the apostles will be subjected to a great trial, but the Lord prays for Peter because it will be his responsibility to be the support of his brethren, in spite of his approaching denial:

> Simon, Simon, behold, Satan has claimed power over you all, so that he can sift you like wheat: but I have prayed for thee, that thy faith may not fail; when, after a while, thou hast come back to me, it is for thee to be the support of thy brethren.

It will be up to him to strengthen the faith of the very apostles.

Finally, we have the important passage in Saint Matthew, the principal parts of which are as follows (XVI, 18 and 19):

> And I tell thee this in my turn, that thou art Peter, and it is upon this rock that I will build my church; and the gates of hell shall not prevail against it; and I will give to thee the keys of the kingdom of heaven; and whatever thou shalt bind on earth shall be bound in heaven, and whatever thou shalt loose on earth shall be loosed in heaven.

Peter is the rock, the foundation on which Christ is going to build his Church, like a building, and the gates of hell, to some the powers of death or, more probably, according to others the powers of evil,[3] shall not prevail

---

(*executio*) the plan of Christ; but the structural authority of governing belongs to Peter alone. See further pages 65, 76, and 97.

[3] In the time of Jesus the Jews understood by hell (Hades) no longer merely the place where the dead dwell, but a place of punishment. See the texts cited in M. J. Lagrange, *Evangile selon saint Matthieu,* 1923, p. 326, who refers particularly to Luke, XVI, 23: ". . . the rich man died too, and found his grave in hell. And there in his suffering, he lifted up his eyes, and saw Abraham far off, and Lazarus in his bosom."

against it. What will the prerogative or gift be which will make Peter a foundation? The following verse tells us: he will receive the power of the keys over the kingdom. Apart from, and more profoundly than, Peter, Christ himself remains the rock and foundation (Acts, IV, 11), that is, the one "who bears the key of David, so that none may shut when he opens, none open when he shuts" (Apoc., III, 7). Both in the case of Peter and in the case of Christ, it should be emphasized, the one who is the foundation and the one who has the keys is the same person.

2. THE PRIVILEGE OF PETER CONCERNS THE STRUCTURE OF THE CHURCH

We now come to the problem of the structure and jurisdictional organization of the Church. Jesus sends it to face the assaults of the powers of hell. He declares that it will be founded on the privilege of Peter, who is to have supreme charge of the keys of the Kingdom and supreme charge of feeding the sheep. If the Church endures:

Either it will maintain the structure which Christ gave it; in that case the person of Peter will die, but the office of Peter will continue. That is what we mean when we say that authority over the universal Church was given to Peter as a personal privilege, which was destined to be handed on to his successors, *in persona propria, non solum pro seipso, sed pro omnibus successoribus suis.*[4] This is the Catholic solution.

Or the Church will exchange the structure which Christ purposely gave it for another structure. This will

4 Cajetan, *op. cit.*, No. 39.

involve a violent break, as if, for example, it were to abandon the charter which the apostles gave it in Scripture. (Holy Scripture belongs to the actual structure of the Church; the apostolic power of writing canonical Scripture no longer belongs to it, but did belong to the nascent Church and disappeared with the apostles.) This break will occur at the death of Peter, or even before. Efforts will be made to explain how this came about, and the effort of Prof. Cullmann will have to be added to so many others. His explanation is offered as a piece of historical reconstruction on a grand scale. Let me make one more observation, however, before considering it.

3. THE PRIVILEGE OF PETER IS A TRANSAPOSTOLIC POWER OF JURISDICTION TO FOUND THE CHURCH IN ACTUAL FACT AND IS, THEREFORE, LASTING

We have just defined the Catholic position. It is very simple. Clouds of dust have been raised against it, but they vanish as soon as we give the words of Christ their real meaning; always subject, of course, to the condition that we believe Jesus to be infallible and to be God. Let us insist for a moment on four important points: Is the privilege of Peter merely apostolic? What is the nature of the succession which hands it on? In what sense does it found the Church? Is it given with a view to being continued?

In the mission of the apostles let us consider the extraordinary, temporary, and non-transmissible charisma which was given to them for the task of building the Church, *respectu Ecclesiae in fieri*, to lay the foundations on Christ. By virtue of this charisma the apostles are enabled to be the eye-witnesses of the death and resurrection of Christ, complete the formulation of the Christian revelation and fix it in the inspired Scriptures, undertake missions, found local churches and incorporate them in the universal Church. This apostolic charisma is common to all the apostles and Peter shares it along with the rest.

But Peter receives in addition a privilege which raises him above the other apostles with respect to one point: in other words a transapostolic privilege. Thenceforth, the apostles can be considered as apostles or legates of Christ, and in this respect they all appear to be substantially equal to each other; [5] or they can be considered as sheep of Christ, entrusted by him to Peter, and in this respect they are not equal to Peter, the vicar of Christ: "Simon, son of John, dost thou care for me more than these others? Yes, Lord, he told him, thou knowest well that I love thee. And he said to him, Feed my lambs" (John, XXI, 15).

What is the purpose of the transapostolic privilege of Peter? In what respect, in what connection is Peter above the other apostles? It is certainly not in connection with witnessing the resurrection of Christ, nor in connection with completing and fixing the deposit of Christian revelation in the inspired Scriptures. It is only in the third connection, that of jurisdiction, that an essential superiority is possible. What is the nature of this jurisdiction? There is only one answer to this question

[5] There is nothing against, and something to be said for, the view that the office of one apostle is superior to that of the others with regard to a given aspect. Thus, the apostolate of Paul is entrusted to him by the risen Christ, not the mortal Christ. His apostolate is superior with regard to this aspect, not substantially or fundamentally. Cajetan, *op. cit.*, No. 28, citing Saint Augustine and Saint Thomas.

and it is the immediately obvious one: In the absence of Christ, who has ascended into heaven, Peter is to become the visible center around which the universal Church is to gather, in which all the local churches founded by the various apostles will be incorporated. For the universal Church, the Spouse and Body of Christ, is one in a unity which is not federative, but organic and mystical. "The Church of God which is at Corinth," according to Saint Paul (I Cor., 1, 2; II Cor., I, 1).[6] The answer to this question must obviously be that the transapostolic privilege of Peter is one with respect to jurisdiction; its object is jurisdictional primacy over the whole Church.[7] That is precisely what the texts say. In the absence of Christ, Peter is the one who will, visibly and excluding all the others, be the shepherd of the sheep, the one who, visibly and excluding all the others, will possess the power of the keys over the Kingdom (John, XXI, 15; Matt., XVI, 19).

In what sense will the transapostolic jurisdictional privilege of Peter enable him to found the Church?

Let us repeat that by virtue of the simple apostolic charisma which he shared with the other apostles Peter could found the Church by witnessing to the death and resurrection of Christ, by completing the deposit of the Christian revelation and by determining this partially in the inspired Scriptures, which will be the charter and constitutional statute of Christians until the end of time,

[6] Cf. the greeting at the beginning of the *Martyrdom of Polycarp:* "The Church of God which sojourns at Smyrna to the Church of God which sojourns at Philomelion, and to all the sojournings (*paroikiai*) of the holy Catholic Church in every place . . ."

[7] According to Saint Thomas the apostolic privilege concerns only the exercise of supreme jurisdictional authority; the transapostolic privilege concerns the possession of supreme jurisdictional authority. See pages 61, 76, and 97.

by spreading the gospel, by establishing local churches and by incorporating these in the universal Church. This was the apostolic charisma which was intended for the building of the Church, *respectu Ecclesiae in fieri.*

But Peter receives in addition from Christ a transapostolic privilege, which is destined to make him, and him alone, the foundation of the Church in another sense, in a new aspect. What is this new aspect? Let us consider what happens in the natural order. One can speak of a person as being the founder of a society or kingdom, if he gathers its members together, gives it a charter or statute, or directs its course in the beginning. A kingdom is founded in this way, as far as its actual establishment or its coming to be is concerned; if it is destined to endure, the person can be said to have founded it *genetically, in a horizontal sense, as far as its origin in the past is concerned.* One can also be the founder of a society or kingdom by being the possessor of the jurisdictional power by which it continues to exist. In such case the person founds the kingdom by being its support, the living rock on which it actually rests; if it is destined to endure, the person can be said to continue founding it, *actually, in a vertical sense, as far as its continuance in the present is concerned.* Passing from the consideration of earthly societies or kingdoms to that of the Church, the Kingdom of Christ, we may say that the apostles found this Kingdom by virtue of their *apostolic* charisma, as far as its establishment or its coming to be is concerned, and, if it is destined to endure, that they are founding it *genetically, in a horizontal sense, and as far as its origin in the past is concerned.* But it is by the transapostolic jurisdictional charisma which was given to Peter alone to the exclusion of the other apostles that he can be said to found the Kingdom in a different sense; he founds it, not as far as its genesis or its coming to be is concerned, but as far as its *present* existence is concerned by being the possessor of the divine authority of jurisdiction by which the Kingdom actually lives, by being the living rock on which the Kingdom rests; and if the Kingdom is to endure, Peter can be said to found it actually, in a vertical sense, and as far as its continuance in the present is concerned. It is one thing to found the Kingdom as far as its origin in the past is concerned, for example, by providing it with the Scriptures; and quite another thing to found the Kingdom as far as its continuance in the present is concerned, by being the living rock on which its divine organic unity rests. It is in this second sense that Peter, visibly and in his capacity as vicar of the absent Christ, founds the Church as a rock which changes its place along with it. Christ in his turn, through Peter, and in a more mysterious manner than Peter, is a living rock from which living waters spring and who changes his location in space and time in order to accompany his people, according to the fine metaphor of Saint Paul: "Let me remind you, brethren, of this. Our fathers . . . all drank the same prophetic drink, watered by the same prophetic rock which bore them company, the rock that was Christ" (I Cor., X, 1-4). The words of Christ concerning Peter's unique role as the foundation of his Church, keeper of the keys, guardian of his Kingdom and shepherd of his sheep, should be re-read with this in mind:

And I tell thee this in my turn, that thou art Peter, and it is upon this rock that I will build my Church, and the gates of hell shall not prevail against it (Matt., XVI, 18). And I will give to thee the keys of the kingdom of heaven (Matt.,

XVI, 19). Simon, son of John, dost thou care for me more than these others? . . . Feed my lambs (John, XXI, 15).

This is what we call the transapostolic privilege of jurisdiction by virtue of which Peter founds the Church, not in a horizontal sense as far as its establishment in the past is concerned, but in a vertical sense as far as its continuance in the present is concerned.

In brief, we may say that a building may be founded in the way that a workman lays the foundation; he may die, but the building will continue to exist. He founds the building in a purely temporal sense, as far as its appearance in the past is concerned.

And a building may be founded with regard to its foundation, on which the weight of the masonry rests; this amounts to founding it structurally, actually, as far as its continued existence in the present is concerned.

All the apostles labored to found the Church in a purely temporal sense according to the first meaning; the privilege of being an apostle involved this.

Peter alone is told that he is the rock on which a Church will rest which will continually be assailed by the powers of hell. This clearly indicates that he is founding the Church structurally according to the second meaning; this is his transapostolic privilege.

Our last question was, Is this privilege given to Peter as something which is destined to last, or will it die with him? Is it given to Peter for himself alone, *solum pro seipso;* or is it given to him for his successors as well, *in se et in persona Ecclesiae*? [8] Protestants say here that there is no mention in the texts either of the notion of duration or of successors. My answer to this is that, if

[8] Cf. Cajetan, *op. cit.*, No. 39; also, *De divina institutione pontificatus totius Ecclesiae in persona Petri apostoli*, Chap. 3.

the notion of duration were truly not mentioned in any way, we doubtless could not say that the privilege of Peter is transmissible; but we could not say that it is not transmissible, either. It would be equally hazardous to give an affirmative or a negative answer. But if the privilege given to Peter by Jesus is not the apostolic charisma of founding the Church in a horizontal sense with regard to its establishment in the past, but the transapostolic charisma of founding the Church in a vertical sense with regard to its continuance in the present, it becomes immediately clear that this privilege is destined to endure according to the mind of Jesus as long as his Church, and that the foundation is destined to last as long as the building. The notion of duration and succession is not explicitly mentioned in the texts, but it is implicitly and truly there. It is necessarily implied in the very nature of Peter's privilege, as soon as this is seen as the foundation of the Church as far as its continuance in the present is concerned, or we may say, as soon as this is seen as a structural privilege in the present. Holy Scripture is also structural in the present; but the privilege of being able to compose Scripture is not structural in the present of the Church, in its *conservari;* it was structural in the past of the Church, in its *fieri.* We may therefore reason as we did above: either the Church will maintain the structure which Christ gave it; in that case the privilege of Peter is synchronous with the Church, it is given to Peter *in persona Ecclesiae*, it is transmissible; or the privilege of Peter is not transmissible, it is not synchronous with the Church, and the structure which Christ solemnly gave it will come tumbling down. It goes without saying that we can reason in this way only if we continue to believe that Christ is the one to whom "all authority in heaven and on earth has been given" and who was not ignorant of the time which would elapse from his resurrection until his second coming, from Pentecost until the *Parousia*.

4. THE TEACHING OF THE VATICAN COUNCIL ON THE PRIMACY OF PETER

Have we clearly indicated the gospel foundation of the Catholic teaching on the primacy of Peter? I believe that we have. The doctrine of the Vatican constitution *De Ecclesia Christi* on the primacy of Peter follows logically from these simple basic notions.

The Prologue [9] to this constitution recalls the intention of Christ to perpetuate the work of our redemption by building the Church, in which, as in the house of the living God, all the faithful shall be united by the bond of one faith and one charity. Hence the great prayer of Christ that they may be one, not only the apostles but those who shall believe in him through their word. The Father sent him and he in his turn sends the apostles, with the intention that there should be shepherds and teachers in the Church until the consummation of the world. In order to ensure unity among the bishops and unity of faith and communion among the faithful,[10] he places at the head of the other apostles blessed Peter, who will be the source and visible foundation of this double unity. The Council then discusses the institution of the primacy, its perpetuation, its nature, and the infallible teaching office.

[9] Denzinger, No. 1821. See pages 45 and 105.
[10] It is evidently a question here not only of canonical communion, but also and above all of the central mystery of communion in charity, in a sacramental and jurisdictional sense.

From the words of Matthew, XVI, 18-20, and John, XXI, 15-17, it follows that Peter "was established by Christ the Lord as prince of the apostles and visible head of the Church militant." [11] What Christ established for the good of the Church, he will preserve until the consummation of the world; it is therefore "through institution by Christ, and according to divine law, that Peter shall perpetually have successors with respect to that which relates to his primacy." [12]

This primacy represents a "plenary and supreme power of jurisdiction over the whole Church," which is not intended to eliminate the jurisdictional power belonging to the bishops, but like the royal power of Christ is intended to support and sustain it.[13]

This power of jurisdiction involves among other functions that of teaching, and if it is to be the foundation for the faith of an infallible Church, against which the gates of hell shall not prevail, it is clear that it must on certain solemn occasions be able to teach infallibly, not with a view to announcing any new revelation, but in order to expound faithfully the deposit of faith which has already been revealed once and for all by the apostles:

> The Roman Pontiff, when speaking solemnly ex cathedra, that is, when carrying out his charge as pastor and teacher of all Christians, he defines by virtue of his supreme apostolic authority the doctrine with regard to faith and morals which ought to be accepted by the universal Church, enjoys, thanks to the divine assistance which was promised to him in the person of blessed Peter, that infallibility with which the divine Redeemer wished to

[11] Denzinger, Nos. 1822-1823.
[12] *Ibid.*, Nos. 1824-1825.
[13] *Ibid.*, Nos. 1826-1831.

provide his Church when it defines doctrine with regard to faith and morals; that is why such definitions of the Roman Pontiff are irreformable by themselves, and not by the consent of the Church.[14]

They are irreformable by reason of the assistance which Christ gives his vicar, not by reason of numbers or the general will; the consent of the Church is still there, not as a founding factor, but as a factor accompanying these definitions.

There is an important fact worth pondering over here. Where in the West do we still find belief in the infallibility of the Church or in the infallibility of Scripture itself? More and more a close connection is becoming apparent between belief in the infallibility of Scripture, its inspiration and its inerrability, and belief in the infallibility of the primacy of Peter.

[14] *Denzinger*, No. 1839.

10

THE PRIVILEGE OF PETER ACCORDING TO THE
VIEW OF PROFESSOR CULLMANN

1. THE GOSPEL TEXT IS AUTHENTIC; IT MEANS THAT THE CHURCH IS TRULY FOUNDED ON THE PERSON OF PETER

Prof. Cullmann recognizes the authenticity of the three Gospel texts of Matthew, Luke, and John, which record the privilege granted to Peter by Jesus. To this extent he agrees with Catholics and differs from the great number of Protestant exegetes who adopt a liberal, modernist, rationalist approach, etc.

It is clear, moreover, that for him Jesus intends to found his Church, not on the faith of Peter as the Reformers maintained, but on the person of Peter himself. He thus differs here from Luther, Calvin, Zwingli, Melancthon, etc., who held that Peter received the title of rock from Jesus as a believer, not as a person, the only rock of the Church being Jesus himself.[1] The thought of Prof. Cullmann is very clear on this point. The text of Saint Matthew

> says that Jesus' role as rock is transferred to a disciple. So there remains only the one possibility, that by this saying Jesus actually meant the person whom he characterized by the name "rock." Indeed, if the saying were referred to the faith of Peter, one could no longer directly discern the connection with the giving of the name, and the saying certainly intends to point to this and even to explain it. The giving of the name, which is an established fact even apart from Matthew, XVI, 17ff., deals with the person of Peter, and not merely with his faith . . . For this reason all Protestant interpretations that seek in one way or another to explain away the reference to Peter seem to me unsatisfactory. No, the fact remains that when Jesus says that he will build his *ekklesia* upon this rock, he really means the person of Simon. Upon this disciple, who in the lifetime of Jesus possessed the specific advantages and the specific weaknesses of which the Gospels speak, upon him who was then their spokesman, their representative in good as well as in bad,[2] and in this sense was the rock of the group of disciples—upon him is to be founded the Church, which after the death of Jesus will continue his work on earth.[3]

[1] In a short work, *De divina institutione pontificatus totius Ecclesiae in persona Petri apostoli*, dedicated to Leo X, dated at Rome, February 17, 1521, and deserving a new edition, Cajetan answers with a remarkable degree of patience and insight those who seem to have taken upon themselves the task of "obscuring the light of the Gospel." He lists their objections one by one, and deals with them clearly and with his usual acumen. It is pleasing to think that before the words of our Lord were inscribed on the dome of Saint Peter's they were examined so calmly and with such learning.

[2] (Msgr. Journet comments here: "I do not understand how Peter can be the representative of Jesus 'in bad.'" He seems to interpret *"son représentant"* as referring to Jesus rather than to the apostles, as Mr. Filson has interpreted it. Translator's note.)

[3] Cullmann, *Peter, Disciple, Apostle, Martyr*, pp. 206-207.

Two anti-Catholic points of view, by far the most frequent, are thus disposed of. On the one hand there is the view of those who accept the genuineness of the Gospel texts, but deny that they have to do with a personal privilege granted to Peter; on the other hand the view of those who do not object to this interpretation, but deny the genuineness of the texts. Nevertheless, in spite of agreement on this important point, Prof. Cullmann does not succeed in escaping from the circle of Protestant interpretation.

I now come to the exegetical and historical portion of his book, in which he attempts to reconstruct in accordance with his own view the picture we ought to form today not only of the life of Peter but of the beginnings of the Church in apostolic times, its nature, its purpose, and the intention of Jesus himself in founding it.

2. THE TRANSAPOSTOLIC POWER OF FOUNDING THE CHURCH STRUCTURALLY IS REFERRED BY PROF. CULLMANN TO THE APOSTOLIC POWER OF FOUNDING THE CHURCH CHRONO-LOGICALLY

The view of a Christ to whom all power has been given in heaven and on earth, master of the passage of time until his second coming, assisting his Church divinely and infallibly, anxious to found it not only with regard to its origin and horizontally in time, but structurally so that it may rest continually on its foundation in a vertical sense, is brushed aside. Instead, we have a view of Christ who "scarcely reckons with a duration of millenniums, but . . . does assume that there will be a rather brief period of time between his resurrection and return." He is concerned to found his Church only with regard to its origin, so that it may have a beginning in time.

Hence it follows that there is no place for a trans-apostolic privilege by virtue of which Peter could found the Church structurally as far as its continuance in the present is concerned. Peter is an apostle like the others. He founds the Church with regard to its origin, as the other apostles do. We have granted ourselves that the apostolic privilege of founding was unique and that it was the same for all,[4] temporary, and non-transmissible. But we have recognized two ways in which the Church could be founded: one, apostolic, as far as its beginning was concerned; the other, transapostolic, as far as its continuance is concerned. For Prof. Cullmann there is only one way, a temporary one. Peter has nothing which the other apostles do not have.

All the promises Jesus made to him:

> And I tell thee this in my turn, that thou art Peter, and it is upon this rock that I will build my Church; and the gates of hell shall not prevail against it (Matt., XVI, 18); . . . but I have prayed for thee, that thy faith may not fail; when after a while thou hast come back to me, it is for thee to be the support of thy brethren (Luke, XXII, 32); . . . Simon, son of John, dost thou care for me more than these others? . . . Feed my lambs. . . . Feed my sheep (John, XXI, 15-17).

—all these promises have in the thought of Jesus only a mere episodic significance. That is the important point for Prof. Cullmann:

[4] *Apostoli inter se possunt comparari dupliciter. Primo in quantum apostoli, et sic omnes fuerunt aequales. Alio modo in quantum oves Christi, ab eo hic corporali conversatione separatae, et sic Petrus solus est pastor."* Cajetan, *De comparatione,* No. 23. See pages 61, 65, 97.

It is not at all arbitrary when in Matthew, XVI, 17ff. we see Peter addressed in his *apostolic capacity* and hence emphasize so strongly the apostolic concept. In any case, the illustration of the building in Ephesians, II, 20, and Revelation, XXI, 14, is connected with the apostolic function, and this is important. So also in Romans, XV, 20, the illustration of the foundation occurs to Paul: "That I may not build upon another foundation." [5]

But this does not prevent the apostles from being the foundation composed of human instruments of God and resting in turn upon Christ; nor does it prevent Peter from having the prominent role among them and for the Church of all later time. *Just as in Ephesians, II, 20, and in Romans, XV, 20, the foundation is to be understood in a chronological way, so also in Matthew, XVI, 17ff.* In Ephesians, II, 20, and Romans, XV, 20, as well as in Revelation, XXI, 14, it nevertheless is impossible, even as a later application, to think of successors of the apostles.[6] *Peter's feeding of the lambs in John XXI, 16ff. is certainly limited by his martyrdom!* So the statement "I will build my *ekklesia*" need not be extended beyond the lifetime of Peter. It could be that at the moment when he gave a promise to Peter in particular, Jesus limited himself to speaking concerning the initial building immediately after his resurrection.[7]

We now have the basis for the different point of view put forth in this book. If pressed, Prof. Cullmann would probably admit that Jesus could foresee a long period of continued existence for his Church, provided it were made clear that the privilege of founding the Church, granted to Peter in Matthew, XVI, 18, is not something which can be handed on:

[5] Cullmann, *op. cit.*, p. 217.
[6] *Loc. cit.*
[7] *Ibid.*, p. 208.

But if we nevertheless assume that *in this first statement* Jesus thought of a period embracing many generations, this does not mean at all that the rock—Cephas—Peter mentioned in this sentence, includes also successors of Peter. In this sentence it is *only the work of building* which belongs to an unlimited future, *not the laying of the foundation of the rock* on which it is built! In the future Jesus will build upon a foundation which is laid in the time of his earthly career and in the time and person of the historical apostle Peter. We shall see that in the entire New Testament the illustration of the foundation, which indeed is identical in meaning with that of the rock, always designates the unique apostolic function, which is chronologically possible only at the beginning of the building; see Ephesians, II, 20; Romans, XV, 20; I Corinthians, III, 10; Galatians, II, 9; Revelation, XXI, 14, 19. In Matthew, XVI, 18, Peter is addressed in his unrepeatable apostolic capacity.[8]

Prof. Cullmann obviously exerts every effort to reduce the transapostolic power of founding the Church structurally in the vertical sense to the apostolic power of founding it in an historical and horizontal sense.

To this our answer must be that the New Testament passages which establish the latter power do not destroy the validity of those which establish the former power.

3. THE INTERPRETATION OF PROF. CULLMANN DESTROYS THE UNITY OF THE PROMISE MADE TO PETER BY JESUS

Prof. Cullmann's preconceptions lead him to a strange conclusion and prevent him from interpreting verse 18 of Matthew XVI: "And I tell thee this in my turn, that thou art Peter, and it is upon this rock that I will build my Church; and the gates of hell shall not prevail

[8] Cullmann, *op. cit.*, pp. 208-209.

against it," with reference to the next verse 19: "And I will give to thee the keys of the kingdom of heaven; and whatever thou shalt bind on earth shall be bound in heaven, and whatever thou shalt loose on earth shall be loosed in heaven."

On the one hand, what is given to Peter in verse 19, namely, stewardship over the Kingdom of heaven and the divine power of binding and loosing, is a power of jurisdiction. No one doubts this. Prof. Cullmann agrees and also holds that certain forms of jurisdictional power are intended to endure as long as the Church, or, in other words, are transmissible.[9] On the other hand, Peter was only given an episodic power of founding the Church in verse 18, which by its very nature cannot be handed on. We must therefore interpret the solemn promise of Jesus to Peter in two separate senses and avoid interpreting the first part with reference to the second part. Peter will doubtless exercise jurisdictional powers among the apostles, but it is not because these functions are jurisdictional and by their nature continuous that they will make him the foundation of the Church, but solely because they are exercised by him in the first days of the Church they will enable him to be called the foundation of the Church in the past:

> To be sure, the sentence concerning the keys, concerning loosing and binding, speaks of functions of the historical Peter that continue in the Church. They refer to church leadership, and this indeed must continue to exist. That, however, does not mean that in this saying in Matthew, XVI, 17ff. Jesus is speaking of the leadership that *later*

---

[9] It is another matter to determine whether the power of jurisdiction which is transmissible also involves an infallible magisterium, or whether the organization of the Church must be seen as a simple human necessity. See above, chaps. VII and VIII.

leaders will give. On the contrary, all that is said here deals with the leadership of him who, according to the preceding sentence, has also the unique mission, absolutely decisive for the Church and not to be repeated, of being the *rock,* of presiding as apostle over the Church immediately after the death and resurrection of Jesus. . . . In what he says Jesus certainly does not exclude the activity of other church leaders in later times. But in this *saying concerning the foundation* he does not speak of them; he speaks of Peter. . . . Jesus will build not upon the keys, nor upon the binding and the loosing, but *upon the apostle Peter,* to whom Jesus *at that time* committed the keys and the binding and loosing." [10]

We have said already that the leadership of the Church by Peter is also *apostolic* leadership, and so belongs to the never to be repeated Rock role, the laying of the foundation. For we dare not forget that the *entire* promise is dominated by the saying about the rock; it indeed, in connection with the giving of the name, forms the point of departure. But on the other hand, we have pointed out many times that in contrast to the office of apostle, that of the leader of the Church continues. Thus we must pay attention to two things: on the one hand, to the non-transferable character of the leadership of the Primitive Church by Peter; on the other hand, to the fact that there must also be leadership later in the Church, so that Peter is in a certain respect the archetype and example for all future church leadership.[11]

4. TWO EXEGETICAL VIEWS

Does this exegesis correspond to the New Testament texts? Perhaps so, when they are read in a certain way which only allows Jesus a single method of founding his Church, namely an historical method as far as its

[10] Cullmann, *op. cit.,* pp. 210-211.
[11] *Ibid.,* pp. 223-224.

beginning is concerned, but not structurally as far as its duration is concerned, when it will be obliged to face all the assaults of the powers of hell; and which, consequently, attempts to resolve the transapostolic privilege of Peter, set forth in the Gospels so forcefully, into the apostolic privilege common to all the apostles. But it is precisely this point of view which we continue to question.

We interpret the Gospel from another, loftier, more suggestive, and more divine point of view. In the very verse in which Jesus announces that he will make Peter alone, and not the other apostles, the foundation of his Church, he declares as a direct consequence of this first choice that the gates of hell, which are to be so active in future generations, will not prevail against it. What divine gift could Peter receive that would enable him to found the Church? He will receive the gift of the keys, he will be the keeper of the keys and steward of the Kingdom of heaven. There can be no doubt that a power of jurisdiction is intended here. He is not told that he will found the Church as an eye-witness of the resurrection of Jesus, or by spreading the gospel, or by completing the deposit of revealed faith and by writing inspired Scripture, or by organizing local churches and incorporating them in the universal Church. He could of course do all these things and found the Church in an apostolic way, as the other apostles could. But he alone is told that he will have the function, over and beyond all that, of founding the Church in a different transapostolic way, by possessing within it the power of the keys.

5. THE APOSTOLIC POWER OF BINDING AND LOOSING AND THE TRANSAPOSTOLIC POWER OF THE KEYS

Somewhat further on in Saint Matthew, XVIII, 18, Jesus addresses all the apostles when he says: "I promise you, all that you bind on earth shall be bound in heaven, and all that you loose on earth shall be loosed in heaven." There is therefore an apostolic power of jurisdiction by which the apostles can found local churches and incorporate them in the universal Church. But these same words were directed to Peter in the singular in XVI, 19: "Whatever *thou* shalt bind on earth shall be bound in heaven; and whatever *thou* shalt loose on earth shall be loosed in heaven." Peter alone was told that he will have the power of the *keys* of the Kingdom of heaven. Peter alone was told that he would be the *rock* on which the Church would be built.

The Gospel therefore compels us to admit two degrees in the jurisdictional power of binding and loosing which God ratifies in heaven: there is the *apostolic* power of jurisdiction common to all the apostles; and a *transapostolic* power of jurisdiction belonging to Peter. Peter is not destined to support the Church against the assaults of the powers of hell by virtue of his *apostolic,* temporary power of jurisdiction, but by virtue of a Christly power of jurisdiction, which is more mysterious and *transapostolic.* Peter is not destined to feed the lambs and sheep of Christ, henceforth hidden from view in divine glory until his second Coming, by virtue of his *apostolic,* temporary, power of jurisdiction, but by virtue of a Christly power of jurisdiction which is more mysterious and *transapostolic.*

6. THE EXTRAORDINARY APOSTOLIC POWER OF BINDING AND
   LOOSING AND THE ORDINARY EPISCOPAL POWER OF BIND-
   ING AND LOOSING

We must make a brief digression here with regard to
Matthew, XVIII, 18.

In addition to the extraordinary and non-transferable
power of jurisdiction of binding and loosing which belonged to the apostles and was destined for the foundation of the Church in the beginning, by virtue of which
each apostle could spread the gospel and organize local
churches, there is an ordinary and transferable power
of jurisdiction over binding and loosing, bequeathed by
the apostles to their successors and intended for the
preservation of the Church in the course of the ages and
the administration of local churches, which is subordinate to the transapostolic authority of Peter. The extraordinary power of jurisdiction is strictly dependent
on the office of apostle; the ordinary power of jurisdiction is only apostolic in the broad sense of the term, and
is co-extensive with the episcopate.[12]

Saint Paul is thinking of the first power, when he
writes to the Romans, XV, 20: "It has been a point of
honor to me to preach the gospel thus, never in places
where Christ's name was already known; I would not
build on the foundation another man had laid . . ."
He is thinking of the second power when he reminds
Titus and Timothy of the privileges and responsibilities
of their pastoral charge.

Prof. Cullmann admits, to be sure, that a period of
"leading" the Church must follow the period of "founding" the Church. But he does not like to speak of suc-

12 Cf. Journet, *L'Eglise du Verbe incarné*, I, pp. 135-162; 463-472.

cessors to the apostles. How could the responsibility of founding the Church in its historical beginning be handed on? How could an apostolate, which is by its very nature something temporary, be continued in an episcopate which is by its very nature permanent? Of course it could not. But we readily perceive where the real difference lies between him and us. Is the deposit of truth revealed infallibly through the exceptional teaching office of the apostles infallibly preserved by the regular teaching office of their successors? Granted that there is necessarily a difference in level between the period of revelation by the apostles, who were inspired, and the period of preservation by their successors, who could only be assisted; does this difference in level nevertheless allow for the actual infallible continuity of the deposit, the *paradosis*? The Catholic Church from its earliest years has maintained that it does.[13] Prof. Cullmann maintains that it does not:

> Elders and bishops certainly do take the place of the apostles, and one may call them successors, even if this expression opens the way to misunderstandings. But in any case it must not be forgotten for a moment that they occupy a completely different position, and they must not be regarded as successors in the sense of "continuers of the apostolic function." They are successors in the chronological sense, but not in their nature. *Their function follows that of the apostles, but as a fundamentally different one.*[14]

Here once again we come to the general problem we have already discussed above.[15] Let us end this digres-

---

[13] See, for example, the passages of St. Irenaeus cited on pp. 57, and 125.

[14] Cullmann, *op. cit.*, p. 219.

[15] In Chapters VII and VIII.

sion, therefore, and return to Prof. Cullmann's explanation of the privilege of Peter.

7. ACCORDING TO PROF. CULLMANN, PETER HAS NO POWER
OTHER THAN WHAT THE OTHER APOSTLES HAVE AND IS
NOT DISTINGUISHED FROM THEM EXCEPT FOR HIS BRIEF
CHRONOLOGICAL PRE-EMINENCE

There are other surprises in store for us along the road on which Prof. Cullmann has embarked.

In our opinion the privilege which Jesus gave Peter of being the rock on which the Church will be founded is a gift so significant, essential, and necessary for the Church, that the latter could not resist the powers of hell without it; this privilege is given to Peter personally, not only for himself, but for all his successors.

In Prof. Cullmann's opinion, on the other hand, it is only a question of the privilege of founding the Church in its historical beginnings, given to Peter no doubt personally, but for him alone, and not extending to his successors.

> Peter, with the other apostles, forms the foundation and yet at the same time constitutes the rock within this foundation. Peter, that is to say, was the *first* who saw the Risen One on Easter. Probably he also received then confirmation of the apostolic commission, and this is the more important since he is the one who had denied Jesus. He accordingly is the apostle *par excellence*. In this essential relation as the outstanding one, he is in a particular way what all the other apostles are. It is interesting to note that here too his position as leader within the apostolic circle rests upon a chronological distinction; *he is the first one who saw the Risen One* . . .[16]

[16] Cullmann, *op. cit.*, p. 218.

It would not be possible to state more clearly that the privilege of Peter is of the same order as that of the other apostles and that it is not transapostolic. It does not even occur to the Professor that the chronological distinction of Peter with respect to his fellow-apostles could come to him from the exceptional dignity which had been promised him—and yet, is not this precisely what the account given in John, XX, 3-10, of the visit of Peter and John to the empty tomb the morning of Easter seems to suggest? On the contrary, according to Prof. Cullmann, it is the chronological distinction of Peter which will cause him to be designated as the head of the apostles.

But only for a short time:

> As far then as the church leadership by Peter is concerned, we must take seriously the fact that the rock apostle led the *entire* Church only at *one* time. That was when, in the days immediately ofter Christ's resurrection and in the days of the giving of the Spirit to the Mother Church in Jerusalem, he stood at its head and exercised the work of binding and loosing, the memory of which the narrative about Ananias and Sapphira has preserved.[17]

> Nevertheless, Peter retains for all time the unique greatness and dignity of having been *in the first days of the Church of Jesus Christ* the leader of the Primitive Church and thereby of the entire Church of that time. This must stand first of all as a fixed fact in the redemptive history at the beginning.[18]

The privilege of Peter, thus reduced to a fleeting role as leader in the beginning, can and still should be revered by Protestant churches:

[17] Cullmann, *op. cit.*, p. 226.
[18] *Ibid.*, p. 224.

It has become the custom to connect the apostle Peter only with the Roman Catholic Church, and the apostle Paul with the Protestant Church. In reality every Church needs also the apostle Peter, because he as "first" among the twelve apostles has to guarantee the continuity with the incarnate Jesus.[19]

The Catholic interpretation is thus disposed of:

When therefore the history of the Primitive Church is invoked to give present significance to the primacy of Peter in relation to leadership over the entire Church, this can happen only in the following way: The Church of today recognizes the redemptive plan of God in the fact that at its initial stage—this really was true at its initial stage—stands the apostle to whom Jesus gave the name "Rock," and to whom he announced that on him he would build his Church.[20]

Christianity is an affair of symbols and memories, nothing more. The mnemic concept is still the only valid one.

8. PETER IS SUPPLANTED BY JAMES IN HIS ROLE AS HEAD OF THE CHURCH, LONG BEFORE COMING TO ROME

Jesus declares in Matthew, XVI, that he will make Peter the rock on which he will establish his Church, which is destined to resist the attacks of hell (verse 18), and that he will give him the keys of the Kingdom of heaven (verse 19); he declares in John, XXI, 15-16, that he will make him the shepherd of his lambs and sheep.

According to Prof. Cullmann all this was realized by the fact that Peter was the first to see the Lord on Easter Day, by his witnessing of the resurrection, and by the

19 Cullmann, *op. cit.*, p. 222.
20 *Ibid.*, p. 226.

fact that he presided over the church of Jerusalem for a short time, when that church was co-extensive with the universal Church. The reign of Peter could only be brief, for the power of being head of the Church has very little connection with that of founding the Church; verse 19, which promises the gift of the keys of the Kingdom, has very little to do with verse 18, which refers to the judicial organization of the Church; in short, the trans-apostolic gift of the keys has so little importance in his estimation that Peter can very quickly be replaced as foundation of the Church in his capacity as head of the church of Jerusalem by James, who from the mere fact that he resides in Jerusalem becomes without further ado the supreme head of the Church.

Nothing appears to be more logical in Prof. Cullmann's opinion. Peter

> . . . stands at the head of the Primitive Church of Jerusalem, though to be sure only in the very earliest time. For James will soon take over the leadership in Jerusalem.[21]

> Only the original Church was led by this apostle, and he led it only in its earliest period. For as soon as the foundation for this leadership is laid, Peter will give it up. Another, James, will take it over in Jerusalem, while Peter will concentrate entirely on his missionary work and will do so, indeed, *in a subordinate role under James.* This later subordination of Peter under James is a fact important in every respect. It confirms first of all that the leadership of the Church by Peter also had its significance for us chiefly as a *starting point.* James is the actual head of the Church from the moment that Peter dedicates himself completely to missionary work. The memory of that fact was steadily retained in the whole of Jewish Chris-

[21] Cullmann, *op. cit.,* p. 224.

tianity, which took an interest in the ancient traditions.[22] He rather subordinates himself to the authority of James as the central government. In a time, therefore, *when Jerusalem continues to hold the leading position* and all other churches—even those founded by Paul, as the collection shows—still look to Jerusalem, Peter himself is dependent on the new leadership in Jerusalem; in Antioch he has to "fear the people who come from James." [23]

Thus, the solemn promise of Jesus concerning the keys of the Kingdom and the power of feeding his lambs and his sheep soon came to nothing. The presence of James in Jerusalem was enough to put an end to it. After a brief period of time Jesus abandoned his chief disciple. Peter simply abdicated and accepted a position subordinate to James, doubtless without feeling that by giving up his function as steward of the Kingdom of heaven and pastor of the sheep of Christ he was betraying his Master a second time.

This is the conclusion at which Prof. Cullmann arrives. We doubt, however, whether all his Protestant readers will be able to follow him this far. But what are they to do then? Must they return to the old dilemma, and maintain, either that the Gospel texts concerning Peter are not genuine, or that they are genuine but do not confer on Peter any transapostolic prerogative of jurisdiction?

9. A TEXT OF FATHER F. M. BRAUN ON THE PROTESTANT EXEGESIS OF "THOU ART PETER"

In a fine work entitled *New Aspects of the Problem of the Church*, in which he examines with a great deal of

22 *Loc. cit.*
23 *Ibid.*, p. 225.

90

calmness and insight the ecclesiological positions of the Protestant school to which Prof. Cullmann belongs, Father Braun, the Catholic exegete, reserves a special excursus under the heading of *Tu es Petrus* for a discussion of some of the explanations of this text proposed by the followers of the new trend. Following a slightly different path, he reaches at the end of his critical analysis the same conclusion we do. According to him the new exegesis

> suppresses the analogy underlying the whole passage in Matthew, XVI, 17-19, between the figurative foundation of the Church represented as a building and the real foundation of the Church as a community, signified further on by the power of the keys. What becomes of the hierarchical nature of the Church and of apostolic succession we can easily imagine. They are simply denied under the pretext that the role attributed to Peter did not belong to the essence of the Church, and, consequently, was not destined to endure. *We therefore see, when all is said and done, between the exegesis of Luther and that of the new trend only a difference of degree.* Both maintain the authenticity and historicity of the text; *both are dominated in their interpretation by the desire to deprive the primacy of the pope of any scriptural basis.* Luther claimed to arrive at this conclusion by maintaining that Matthew XVI, 17-19, did not apply to Peter. Too well-versed to believe in this impossible exegesis, the representatives of the new trend take their own revenge, and thus succeed in remaining faithful to the thought of the Reformer in his opposition to the Church of Rome by granting Peter only a personal prerogative, which is strictly non-transferable.[24]

[24] F. M. Braun, O.P., *Aspects nouveaux du problème de l'Eglise* (Fribourg, 1942), pp. 97-98. (Italics mine).

10. THE PROBLEM OF THE SURVIVAL OF JEWISH RITES AMONG THE CHRISTIANS AND THE REBUKE OF PAUL TO PETER, ACCORDING TO THE CATHOLIC VIEW

In submitting to James, Peter is represented as submitting to one who had favored the promotion of schismatical tendencies in the Church. In our opinion this notion put forth in Prof. Cullmann's book will not only be received by Catholics and Orthodox but by many Protestants who share our belief in the sanctity of the primitive Church as an extremely improbable interpretation of the events, and even a scandalous one.

We have no intention of minimizing the importance of the dispute which developed during the first years of the Church between the Gentile Christians, whom Saint Paul taught to commend themselves solely to Christ and his grace, and certain Jewish Christians who were active in propagating the notion that it was still necessary to follow Jewish observances after baptism and that the gospel would not be of any use unless circumcision and other practices of the law were also observed. The latter were a disturbing element in the Christian communities founded by Paul, and attempted to create a schism by keeping Jews and Greeks separate in the Catholic Church, which ought to know neither Jew nor Greek.

The Church was doubtless going through a critical phase at this time which could have been fatal to it, if it had not been held in check and divinely assisted by the apostles. What was their teaching, what kind of leadership did they impose on the Church, and what attitude did they adopt with regard to circumcision and the other observances of the Old Law?

The famous controversy on this point between Saint

Jerome and Saint Augustine is well known, in which the former admitted defeat and the latter showed the true scope of his genius and magnanimity.[25] The Old Law remained binding and retained its validity until the time of Christ's passion. An indication of this can be seen in the fact that the infant Jesus is circumcised the eighth day after his birth (Luke, II, 21); he is presented in the Temple (Luke, II, 22); he later sends the lepers to the priests (Mark, I, 44); and himself goes up to celebrate the Feast of Tabernacles (John, VII, 10). With the passion of Christ all this is changed and it becomes necessary to regard the observances of the Old Law in a new light. The difficulty arises from the fact that the same apostles, Peter and Paul for example, are found teaching that the Old Law has been abrogated, while they continue to sanction the observance of it under certain circumstances. This is the precise point at issue between Jerome and Augustine.

Jerome thought that the ceremonies of the Law became pernicious and deadly immediately after the passion for all those to whom the grace of the New Testament had been sufficiently explained. Henceforth, he maintained, when the apostles themselves respected the usages of the Law from fear of scandalizing Christians who had been converted from Judaism, for example, when Peter forced the baptized Gentiles to observe Jewish practices (Gal., II, 14), when Paul circumcised Timothy (Acts, XVI, 3), and when James and the Council of Jerusalem ordered the converted Gentiles to observe certain precepts (Acts, XV, 29), they did so, not by reason of any divine dispensation, as some of the

[25] Saint Augustine, *Epist.*, LXXXII, 14-22. Summarized in Saint Thomas, *S. Th.*, I-II, Q. 103, a. 4, ad 1 et 2, Vol. I, pp. 1086-1087.

Fathers had held, but as a sort of gesture of conformity, performing the rites of the Law for reasons which were themselves unknown to the Law, for example, circumcision for hygienic reasons, etc. Such a course of action, however, was certainly destined to mislead Christians and was unworthy of the apostles of truth; even those who thought that the apostles acted this way by reason of a divine dispensation could not avoid the unpalatable conclusion that, if this latter explanation were offered, it would follow that Paul had had no real reason for rebuking Peter at Antioch (Gal., II, 14), and that he would only have seemed to oppose him in a sort of feigned way which would have been inconsistent with the character of such an apostle.

Hence it is the solution of Saint Augustine which prevails. He holds that after the death and resurrection of the Savior the ceremonies of the Law were dead and of no avail for those to whom the faith had been revealed, but in such a way that they could be followed for a while by the Jews without danger of sin—or even by the Gentiles who had been converted to the faith—provided that they did not place their hopes in these observances. The apostles could occasionally observe these practices, and if they actually did so, it was in order to indicate that they were not abandoning the Old Law which had served them so well and which Jesus himself had observed, as one would give up the practices of idolatry. According to the famous phrase of Saint Augustine, they showed as much piety in conducting the Synagogue to its tomb, as there would be impiety today if anyone thought of stirring up the dormant ashes and violating the sepulcher of these rites. *Et ideo hoc modo erat Mater Synagoga deducenda ad tumulum cum honore,*

94

as Saint Thomas says, summing up the thought of Saint Augustine.[26]

How long could the ceremonies of the Old Law be observed in this way without danger of sin? Saint Augustine does not fix any time limit, but is content to refer to the first years of the Church when the Christian faith was being revealed. Saint Thomas specifies as limiting dates the passion of Christ and the spreading of the gospel. Perhaps the destruction of Jerusalem should be taken as the official sign of the final rejection of the synagogue and the abrogation of the Old Law. By then Rome had already been consecrated by the martyrdom of its two apostles.

Two questions thus presented themselves to the apostles. The first is a dogmatic question, whether the ceremonies of the Old Law lost all their saving efficacy after the death of Christ. Anyone who continued to place his hopes in them and at the same time in the blood of Christ would misunderstand the fundamental truth of Christianity. All the apostles agreed in deciding this first question in the same way. There is no suggestion of a division among them here. "It is by the grace of our Lord Jesus Christ that we hope to be saved," Peter tells the Council of Jerusalem. He expresses on this occasion the thought of Barnabas, Paul, and James. James does not belong to the circle of the pro-Jewish pharisees, but to that of the apostles (Acts, XV, 11-29). When attacked by the pro-Jewish faction which was disturbing the Galatians, Paul is anxious to prove to the latter that he has compared his doctrine with that of the apostles:

[26] Saint Thomas, *IV Sent.*, d. 1, q. 2, a. 5, ad. 3.

Then, when three years had passed, I did go up to Jerusalem, to visit Peter, and I stayed a fortnight there in his company; but I did not see any of the other apostles, except James, the Lord's brother. Such is my history; as God sees me, I am telling you the plain truth (Gal., I, 18-20).

Then after an interval of fourteen years, once again I went up to Jerusalem with Barnabas, and Titus also accompanied me. I went up in obedience to a revelation, and there I communicated to them (*only in private, to men of repute*) the gospel I always preach among the Gentiles; *was it possible that the course I had taken and was taking was useless?* And it is not even true to say that they insisted on my companion Titus, who was a Greek, being circumcised; we were only thinking of those false brethren who had insinuated themselves into our company so as to spy on the liberty which we enjoy in Jesus Christ, meaning to make slaves of us. To these we did not give ground for a moment by way of obedience; we were resolved that the true principles of the gospel should remain undisturbed in your possession. *But as to what I owe to those who were of some repute*—it matters little to me who or what they were, God makes no distinction between man and man—these men of repute, I say, *had nothing to communicate to me. On the contrary, those who were reputed to be the main support of the Church, James, Cephas, and John . . . recognizing the grace God had given men . . . joined their right hands in fellowship with Barnabas and myself;* the Gentiles were to be our province, the circumcised theirs.[27] Only we were to remember the poor; which was the very thing I had set myself to do. (Gal., II, 1-7, 9-10).

The most careful examination of these texts would never reveal that with regard to this first question, from the dogmatic point of view, there was any disagreement

[27] On the meaning of this decision, see further page 100.

between the apostles, or that one of the apostles had entertained heretical or schismatical views.

The second question relates not to dogma, but to prudence. The rites of the Old Law no longer have any validity, but Jesus observed them; they may therefore be allowed to survive for a time, provided they are not the occasion for misunderstanding or scandal. The attitude to be adopted will and must vary according to the circumstances. It happened that Peter had been wrong in condoning the practices of those who had been converted from Judaism at Antioch and was rebuked for this by Paul from considerations of prudence:

> Afterwards, when Cephas came to Antioch, I made an open stand against him; he stood self-condemned. He had been eating with the Gentiles, until we were visited by certain delegates from James; but when these came, he began to draw back and hold himself aloof, overawed by the supporters of circumcision. The rest of the Jews were no less false to their principles; Barnabas himself was carried away by their insincerity. So, when I found that they were not following the true path of the gospel, I said to Cephas in front of them all, Since thou, who art a born Jew, dost follow the Gentile, not the Jewish way of life, by what right dost thou bind the Gentiles to live like Jews? (Gal., II, 11-14).

If Peter errs, it is not in observing the customs of the Old Law; this he could have done since he was a Jew; it is by scandalizing the Gentile Christians from fear of scandalizing the Christian Jews.[28]

There is no suggestion in these passages that when Peter fears the delegates of James, it is because he has been deprived of the power of the keys received from

---

[28] S. Th., I-II, Q. 103, a. 4, ad. 2, Vol. I, p. 1087.

the hands of Jesus, or that he has subordinated himself to James, or that James has become the head of the universal Church.

Paul opposes Peter regarding a matter of opportuneness. He had himself made concessions to the Old Law on other occasions, for example when Timothy was circumcised. But at the present time he is convinced that a concession would be disastrous and would compromise the work of converting the Gentiles. By what right does Paul oppose Peter? He opposes him regarding a matter which concerns the organization of the church at Antioch and missionary work among the Gentiles. This field belonged to the extraordinary jurisdictional power which all the apostles had been given as apostles. On this level, Paul was the equal of Peter. Saint Thomas declares that Paul was the equal of Peter with regard to the carrying out of supreme jurisdictional power; that was a strictly apostolic privilege. But Paul was not equal to Peter with regard to the structural possession of supreme jurisdictional power; this is the special transapostolic privilege of Peter.[29]

11. ACCORDING TO PROF. CULLMANN THE APOSTOLIC CHURCH IS ABANDONED BY CHRIST AND RENT BY SCHISM

In the Catholic view it is the dogmatic unity of the apostles which saves the Church from schism and catastrophe during its first years. Prof. Cullmann views this period in a different light.

We may remember that Paul explains to the Galatians,

---

[29] *"Dicendum est quod apostolus (Paulus) fuit par Petro in executione auctoritatis, non in auctoritate regiminis."* Saint Thomas, *Comm. ad Gal.* II, 11. See above pages 61, 65, and 76.

98

II, 7, 9, that agreement was reached at the Council
of Jerusalem that he and Barnabas should be sent to the
Gentiles, while James, Cephas, and John are to have
the circumcised as their province:

> . . . those who were reputed to be the main support of
> the Church, James, Cephas and John . . . recognizing
> the grace God had given me . . . joined their right hands
> in fellowship with Barnabas and myself; the Gentiles
> were to be our province, the circumcised theirs.

Nothing more is needed to suggest to Prof. Cullmann
that there was a definite schism among the apostles.

> The bond created by the collection was the more neces-
> sary because now, as a result of the agreement reached
> at Jerusalem, there were two missionary organizations.
> According to Galatians, II, 9, this was the decision of
> the apostles reached in Jerusalem: *Paul and his fellow
> workers were to go to the Gentiles, while the missionaries
> from Jerusalem went to the circumcised.* Thus there oc-
> curred even in Primitive Christianity a decisive church
> split [*schisme ecclésiastique définitif*], even though it
> took place in a peaceful way. In opposition to the later
> divisions, especially the great ones which go back to the
> sixteenth century Reformers, this first one, in spite of the
> complete and mutually recognized independence, never-
> theless expressed the common bond in that joint task of
> the collection.[30]

This last remark is further developed in a note:

> . . . we of course do not mean that the situation today
> is the same as it was at the time of the Apostolic Council.
> The gulf between the two separated Churches is unfor-
> tunately very much deeper. For here the division has not
> taken place in peace and "with a handshake," as it did in
> Jerusalem. Nevertheless, there too, in that Primitive

[30] Cullmann, *op. cit.*, p. 44.

Christian discussion concerning circumcision, what was involved was a doctrinal, *unbridged* difference, which concerned a *central point,* that is, the conception of grace. In this important respect, as the actual separation and the continued doctrinal discussion on this theme in the letters of Paul show, the discussion even on that occasion did not issue in a shared conviction. If nevertheless the decision to undertake separate labors was made *"with a handshake,"* this fact should give us food for thought even today.[31]

Such is the ". . . Church in all its beauty, no stain, no wrinkle, no such disfigurement . . . holy . . . spotless" (Eph., V, 27); which is ". . . God's household . . . the Church of the living God, the pillar and foundation upon which the truth rests," (I Tim., III, 15); to which Jesus gave the assurance that the gates of hell would not prevail against it (Matt., XVI, 18); of which the "Apostles and prophets are the foundation on which you were built, and the chief corner-stone of it is Jesus Christ himself" (Eph., II, 20). Such is the Church which begins to totter as soon as it expands beyond Jerusalem; it comes crashing down and splits in two.

Such are the apostles for whose continued unity Jesus had prayed: "Holy Father, keep them true to thy name, thy gift to me, that they may be one, as we are one" (John, XVII, 11). Such are the ones to whom he had promised his continual and everlasting assistance:

All authority in heaven and on earth . . . has been given to me; you, therefore, must go out, making disciples of all nations, and baptizing them in the name of the Father, and of the Son, and of the Holy Ghost, teaching them to observe all the commandments which I have given you. And behold I am with you all through the days that are

[31] Cullmann, *op. cit.*, p. 44.

coming, until the consummation of the world (Matt., XXVIII, 18-20).

Such are the apostles who, shortly after the graces of Pentecost have been poured out on them, rend with their own hands the sacred unity of the Church, and then strive to fit the pieces together again by setting up a welfare organization.

This school has no qualms about enumerating all these disasters, for they must show at all costs how mistaken the views of those are who find in Scripture, along with all its divine promises, that Peter is the permanent foundation of the Church.

What did the decision of the Council of Jerusalem, which sent Paul to the Gentiles and the other apostles "to the circumcised," really mean? When Paul recalls this decision to the attention of the Galatians, II, 9,[32] he does not intend in the slightest way to oppose the mission to the Gentiles to the mission to the circumcised, as if they were entirely independent of one another.

He knew through his own experience that the distinction between Jew and Gentile was not an absolute one. The reason why he emphasizes this distinction so clearly, and mentions it three times (Gal., II, 7-9) is because this is the decision which was actually reached at Jerusalem; past experience was taken as an example and guide for the future, but was not intended to interfere with the apostles' freedom of action or the grace of God. There is no reason to think that Paul later on, contrary to his own practice as Loisy would have it, thought up *the idea of two radically distinct apostolates, independent of one another and without any relation except the remote one of charity.* We must also recognize that *circumcision* did not have

[32] There is good reason to believe that Acts XV, 4, and Gal., II, 1, refer to the same occasion, in spite of minor differences.

the same meaning then as it does today. . . . There was a Jewish nation at that time, although not an independent state, as the center of the *diaspora* spread over the whole Roman world, and the term *circumcision* was applied especially to this nation at the time of the spreading of the gospel to distinguish it from the Gentiles. Paul renounces any intention of preaching to the Jews in Palestine, and abstained from encroaching upon the preserve of James; the apostles at Jerusalem, especially as long as James is at their head, will concentrate on spreading the gospel in Palestine. *But the mission of Peter is universal,* and Paul will not be surprised to find him at Antioch, while he himself is preaching to the Jews who are scattered among the Gentiles.[33]

When he comes to the difference of opinion at Antioch Prof. Cullmann writes:

This however means that in principle Paul was independent not only of the Mother Church in Jerusalem—toward which, however, he had the obligation of the collection—but especially of Peter. So we understand that when the conflict concerning table fellowship with converted Gentiles occurred at Antioch (Gal., II, 11ff.), Peter does not appear in any sense as Paul's superior, but on the contrary *must accept a rebuke from him.* It may be that the Reformers, in their polemic against Rome, emphasized much too strongly the significance of this reprimand of Peter. On the other hand, even the Church Fathers recognized its importance.[34] It may also be correct that Paul, in spite of this conflict, did not cease to designate Simon by his title Cephas, Rock.[35] Nevertheless, this passage

[33] M. J. Lagrange, O.P., *Epitre aux Galates* (Paris, 1918), p. 38. (Italics mine).

[34] We have seen how they resolved the problem.

[35] Father F. M. Braun, O.P., in *Aspects nouveaux du problème de l'Eglise,* p. 88, points out the importance of the different marks of deference which Paul shows toward Peter: "The fact that in Gal., I, 18; II, 9, 11, 14; I Cor., I, 12; III, 22; IX, 5; XV, 5, Peter is called Cephas is certainly not without its significance."

proves that from the time when each begins to exercise his parallel mission, no one can speak of a "primacy" of Peter in relation to Paul . . .[36]

To represent Peter as forced to "accept a rebuke from him" amounts to forcing the meaning of this passage. Paul writes: "Afterwards, when Cephas came to Antioch, I made an open stand against him" (Gal., II, 11). To make an open stand against is to speak to someone else, not as a superior bringing pressure to bear on an inferior, but as equal to equal. The attitude of Paul is explained by what we have already said, following the interpretation of the great theologians, with regard to the equality of the apostles as apostles, especially with regard to the spreading of the gospel and the organization of local churches. This equality does not annul the effect of the promise of Jesus at all. It does not affect the transapostolic privilege of Peter. How could anyone imagine, much less, that it could ever serve to stir up schismatic opposition among the apostles?

It is worth noting that the interpretation which enables Prof. Cullmann to avoid admitting that Peter enjoyed a continual primacy also leads him to the conclusion that the apostolic Church was rent by schism. Would it be going too far to see in this kind of interpretation the fitting judgment of God on Protestantism? We merely pose the question.

[36] Cullmann, op. cit., pp. 46-47.

11

THE PRINCIPLE OF SUCCESSION
ACCORDING TO THE CATHOLIC VIEW

1. BY ESTABLISHING HIS SEE AT ROME PETER UNITES HIS PRIMACY OVER THE UNIVERSAL CHURCH WITH THE OFFICE OF BISHOP OF ROME

According to the Catholic view, when Peter arrives in
Rome, he is already, by virtue of the irrevocable, omnip-
otent promise of his Master, the foundation which is
intended to support the Church against the assaults of
hell, the steward of the Kingdom of heaven, the visible
pastor Christ left behind for his lambs and sheep, in
short, Christ's vicar over the Church, the possessor of
a transapostolic pontifical authority over the whole
Church.

Accordingly, when he comes to Rome to establish not
only his place of residence (*locus*) but his see (*sedes*)—

104

or his chair (*cathedra*)—as James had established his residence and see at Jerusalem, the office of bishop of Rome and the universal transapostolic pontifical authority which he possesses will not continue to exist in him side by side; the person of Peter will not embody two pontifical authorities in act, but only in potentiality,[1] for the office of bishop of Rome will be absorbed in the universal, transapostolic pontifical office, in such a way that the same pontiff will henceforth be Roman pontiff and universal pontiff by virtue of one pontifical office or authority.

If it has been revealed that the Church is to rest actually, structurally, and vertically, until the consummation of the world on the foundation of Peter and on the chain of his successors—since the foundation is destined to last as long as the building—it is implicitly revealed at the same time, by virtue of the exceptional privilege which was destined to cease with his death, that Peter could determine the conditions which would enable the chain of his successors to be recognized. By uniting in an indissoluble manner the office of bishop of Rome and the universal transapostolic pontifical office Peter made clear to the future Church in a precise way where the chain of his successors was to be found. This fusion of the two pontifical offices, this absorption of the first in the second, appears as a dogmatic fact.[2]

Let us make careful note that *residence* is one thing, and *see* another. The residence can be transferred elsewhere, for example when it was transferred to Avignon; but the pope remains bishop of Rome. If Rome were

---

[1] Cajetan, *De divina institutione pontificatus* . . . , Chap. 13.
[2] Cf. Journet, *L'Eglise du Verbe incarné,* I, pp. 522-530, where this point is further discussed.

destroyed, the successors of Peter would remain *de jure* bishops of Rome, and would not cease to be so *de facto*, simply because the city of Rome, or the church which is at Rome, had ceased to exist.

2. THE TEACHING OF THE VATICAN COUNCIL ON THE CONTINUANCE OF THE PRIMACY OF PETER IN THE ROMAN PONTIFFS

In its *Dogmatic Constitution on the Church of Christ*, Session IV, Chap. 2, the Vatican Council considers the continuance of the primacy of Peter in the Roman pontiffs and begins by referring to the Council of Ephesus, thus:

> There can be no doubt for anyone, and all the ages have firmly believed, that holy and blessed Peter, prince and head of the apostles, pillar of the faith and foundation of the Catholic Church, received the keys of the kingdom of heaven from our Lord, Savior, and Redeemer, Jesus Christ; and that he continues to this very day to live, preside and exercise judgment through his successors, the bishops of the see of Rome, founded by him and consecrated by his blood; in such a way that whoever succeeds Peter in this chair receives by the institution of Christ himself the primacy of Peter over the whole Church.[3]

The canon defining the Catholic faith on this point is worded thus:

> If anyone says that it is not by divine institution of Christ the Lord, that is, by divine right, that blessed Peter has continual successors in his primacy over the universal Church, or that the Roman pontiff is not the successor of blessed Peter in this primacy, let him be anathema.[4]

[3] Denzinger, No. 1824.
[4] *Ibid.*, No. 1825. See pages 44, and 70.

3. THE "HISTORICAL" CERTAINTY OF PETER'S COMING TO ROME AND THE CERTAINTY "OF FAITH" THAT HE ESTABLISHED HIS SEE THERE

We believe that Peter came to Rome and that he died there as a martyr. This is an historical fact which historians of the origins of Christianity, and most recently Prof. Cullmann, no longer question. The Vatican Council refers to this historical fact when it says, in an incidental connection which does not appear in the final definition, that Peter not only founded, but "consecrated" the church of Rome "with his blood."

But the indissoluble union of the office of the bishop of Rome and the universal transapostolic pontifical office and authority is a dogmatic fact for us, which history of course can never contradict, but which at the same time it can never establish, and which depends on a certitude higher than that of history; this is how we believe in the divinity of Christ who founds his Church structurally on Peter so that it may endure until the consummation of the world, and how we believe that the transapostolic mission of Peter will continue after his death.

Even if in some impossible way history could prove that Peter had never come to Rome, it would still not upset the dogmatic fact of which we are speaking. It would be sufficient for Peter, wherever he happened to be, to have decreed that his transapostolic pontifical authority over the universal Church should be transferred to Rome. That is a spiritual fact which could take place at a distance. Soloviev has well said:

> We might even admit that Peter never went personally to Rome and yet at the same time from the religious point

of view maintain a spiritual and mystical transmission of his sovereign authority to the bishop of the Eternal City. . . . The mighty spirit of St. Peter, guided by his Master's almighty will, might well seek to perpetuate the center of ecclesiastical unity by taking up his abode in the center already formed by Providence and making the bishop of Rome heir of his primacy.[5]

This does not mean that we are underestimating the importance of history, nor does it amount to a view, as some would have us believe, which ". . . completely surrenders the appeal to the history of the historical Peter." [6] It only amounts to establishing a hierarchy of values among the different kinds of certitude: that of history, that of apologetics, and that of faith.[7]

4. CATHOLICISM DOES NOT CONFUSE OR SEPARATE FAITH AND REASON; IT DISTINGUISHES THEM IN ORDER TO HAR-MONIZE THEM

We ought once and for all to stop confusing the certainty of faith, which is divine, with the certainty of credibility, which is human. These two must neither be confused nor separated, but should be distinguished from each other so that they may be harmonized; the whole Catholic position depends upon keeping this distinction clear.

We believe by divine *faith* that the primacy of Peter is continued in the Roman pontiffs.

Historical research may: a) establish the existence of this belief in the early Church; b) it may even establish in accordance with its own methods the fact that

[5] Vladimir Soloviev, *Russia and the Universal Church*, translated by Herbert Rees (London: Geoffrey Bles, Ltd., 1948), p. 121.
[6] Cullmann, *Peter, Disciple, Apostle, Martyr*, p. 232.
[7] Journet, *op. cit.*, I, p. 524.

Peter came to Rome and died there. It can never by itself arrive at any conclusions which are more than *human* certitudes or probabilities.

Divine or mystical certainty, properly speaking, could never rest on certitude or probability which is merely human and rational. Or, to put it another way, it could "rest" on them only in the way in which the sun's rays rest on the earth, the way a ship's ladder rests on the waves. The certitudes of faith are based on the prevenient action of God and his grace on the human soul: "See where I stand at the door knocking; if anyone listens to my voice and opens the door, I will come in to visit him, and take my supper with him, and he shall sup with me" (Apoc., III, 20). They are based on the inner, mystical attestation of God in us: "The man who believes in the Son of God has this divine attestation in his heart" (I John, V, 10). Such a man is born of God; he is greater than the world and its certitudes: "Whatever takes its origin from God must needs triumph over the world; our faith, that is the triumphant principle which triumphs over the world. He alone triumphs over the world, who believes that Jesus is the Son of God" (I John, V, 4-5).

The certitudes of faith are not rational, much less irrational; they are superrational.

The certitudes of history and apologetics, and the certitudes of credibility, are rational. They inform us that it is not unreasonable, but rather supremely reasonable, to believe superrational mysteries of faith; and that, conversely, it is unreasonable not to believe them.

> Our religion is wise and foolish. Wise, because it is the most learned and the most founded on miracles, prophecies, etc. Foolish, because it is not all this that causes us to belong to it; this makes us indeed condemn those who

are not of it, but is not the cause of belief in those who
are. It is the Cross that makes them believe, *ne evacuata
sit crux.*[8]

Many passages could be cited from Pascal on this
theme.[9]

Divine and human things, certitude of faith and of
reason, supernatural judgment of belief and natural
judgment of credibility: once again it must be said that
these must not be confused, and at the same time they
must not be separated. They must be distinguished and
harmonized. It is not a question either of the fideism of
the Reformers, or of the rationalism of liberal Protestants, but of two unequal gifts of God to men: divine
faith and human reason. This is the teaching of the Vatican Council.[10]

5. HOW DID IT COME ABOUT THAT KNOWLEDGE OF THE PRIMACY OF PETER, WHICH WAS ALWAYS A LIVING REALITY AT ROME, BECAME OBSCURED IN CERTAIN PARTS OF CHRISTENDOM?

While Peter alone possessed the structural transapostolic
power of governing the universal Church, the other
apostles possessed along with him, although still in an
extraordinary manner, the executive power to found
missions and local churches. In this important respect
they were therefore his equals, and his prerogative could
therefore appear to a certain extent limited and neutral-
ized, or rather, overshadowed, by theirs.

This explains not only why Saint Paul or Saint James
could act with such freedom, but also why the jurisdic-

[8] Pascal, *Pensées*, p. 187.
[9] This is one of the important secondary themes stressed in my book on Pascal, *Vérité de Pascal* (Saint-Maurice, 1951).
[10] Denzinger, Nos. 1795-1800.

tional primacy which first belonged to Peter and was then transmitted to his successors in the Roman see was not called upon to manifest certain of its potentialities from the very beginning. Pope Saint Clement was contemporary with Saint John the Apostle.

This also explains why, in spite of the fact that the awareness of the primacy always remained a living reality at Rome, it seems that in the churches which were outside the orbit of Rome's immediate influence—this at least is the impression we get from the letters of Saint Ignatius, the writings of Saint Cyprian and those of the Cappadocians later on—it was believed that because the bishops were the successors of the apostles it was possible to pass without any difference or distinction of level from the government of the apostles to the government of the bishops; as if it were sufficient for the bishops to agree among themselves to be able to realize that unity which the apostles had assured to the universal Church in their lifetime. This is the source of a certain amount of misunderstanding, for the apostles had received in addition to the simple authority of a bishop an extraordinary power of government which was not destined to be handed on to the bishops, but which after their deaths was to be handed over to the jurisdictional primacy of Peter and his successors.[11]

6. THE PROMISE OF JESUS "FOUNDS" THE SUBSEQUENT PRE-
SIDING ROLE OF THE ROMAN CHURCH, AND THIS PRESID-
ING ROLE "REALIZES" OR FULFILLS THE PROMISE

If we believe that Jesus is God, the promise which he made to Peter to found on him the Church which is des-

[11] Cf. Journet, *L'Eglise du Verbe incarné*, I, pp. 580-582.

---

tined to prevail against the city of evil, to give him the keys of his Kingdom, and to establish him as pastor of his lambs and sheep, cannot be illusory.

We must therefore ask how the prophecy of Jesus actually came to be fulfilled. What episcopal see has defended throughout the ages in the East as well as in the West the divinity of Christ, the divine inspiration of Holy Scripture, the supreme value of revelation, and the mystery of the divine and organic unity of the Church?

With reference to these things it is the church of Rome which obviously corresponds to the prophecy of Jesus. At the same time, conversely, the church of Rome is the one which fulfills the prophecy of Jesus, in the way in which the fulfillment of a prophecy always and at all times fulfills the prophecy. There is no vicious circle here.

7. A PASSAGE OF VLADIMIR SOLOVIEV ON THE RELATIONS BETWEEN THE PROMISE OF CHRIST AND THE SEE OF PETER AT ROME

I wish to quote here a passage from Soloviev which I have already cited in *The Church of the Word Incarnate*: [12]

The perfect circle of the Universal Church requires a unique center, not so much for its perfection as for its very existence. The Church upon earth, called to gather in the multitude of nations, must, if she is to remain an active society, possess a definite universal authority to set against *national divisions;* if she is to enter the current of history and undergo *continual change and adaptation* in her external circumstances and relationships and yet preserve her identity, she requires an authority essentially

[12] Journet, *L'Eglise du Verbe incarné*, I, p. 591.

conservative but nevertheless active, fundamentally unchangeable though outwardly adaptable; and finally, if she is set amid the frailty of man to assert herself in reaction against all the powers of evil, she must be equipped with an absolutely firm and impregnable foundation stronger than the gates of hell. Now we know on the one hand that Christ *foresaw the necessity* of such a monarchical principle and therefore conferred on a single individual supreme and undivided authority over this Church; and on the other hand we see that *of all the ecclesiastical powers in the Christian world there is only one which perpetually and unchangingly preserves its central and universal character;* and at the same time is especially connected by an ancient and widespread tradition with him to whom Christ said: "Thou art Peter, and it is upon this rock that I will build my Church; and the gates of hell shall not prevail against it." *Christ's words could not remain without their effect in Christian history and the principal phenomenon in Christian history must have an adequate cause in the word of God.* Where then have Christ's words to Peter produced a corresponding effect except in the chair of Peter? Where does that chair find adequate cause except in the promise made to Peter? [13]

The prophecy is the cause of its fulfillment, and the fulfillment, which is the effect of the prophecy, explains it retrospectively. There is no vicious circle here.

8. ANSWER OF VASILIJ ROSANOV TO DOSTOIEVSKI AND THE SLAVOPHILS

Father Tyszkiewicz, S.J., has just published a translation of important passages from the works of Vasilij Rosanov (1856-1919), which have a bearing on Catholicism.[14] I

[13] Soloviev, *op. cit.,* p. 107 (Italics mine).

[14] S. Tyszkiewicz, S.J., "Réflexions du penseur russe V. Rosanov sur le catholicisme," *Nouvelle Revue de Théologie* (Dec., 1952), pp. 1062-1074.

wish to cite here those portions which concern the primacy of Peter, which Rosanov defends against Dostoievski and the Slavophils.

In an appendix to his book *The Legend of the Grand Inquisitor of F. M. Dostoievski*, in which he cites long, anti-Catholic passages taken from the different works of Dostoievski, Rosanov adds:

> All that as a resumé of the facts may perhaps be fair enough. But we cannot close our eyes to the last part of the words spoken by Christ, as they are to be found in the last chapter of the Gospel of Saint John: "Feed . . ." That is the origin of the authority against which Dostoievski rages in vain, a one-person, exceptional and not at all collective authority, for this very significant word was not addressed to the group of the apostles. . . . Can we conceive of any limits being set on the development in the past or the development in the future of this last testament of the Savior, which is so clearly emphasized by being repeated three times, and—this is the most important thing—just before he ascended into heaven? These words are truly like the mantle which Elias threw to Eliseus . . . The Church was, is, and always will be a golden dome, crowned by a lantern, and will never be the flock of Chigalev. It possesses authority, is hierarchic, and pyramidal in form; a pyramid of course has an apex. Dostoievski's babbling about some kind of *authentic Christianity* or *pure Orthodoxy* which he has allegedly discovered, is basically a reactionary return to the old and glorified world of the Slavs . . . to the old principle of Veles and Daj-Bog (pagan gods).

In a chapter entitled "Why all this furor?" in his book *Close to the Walls of the Church*, Rosanov addresses his remarks to the Slavophils:

> 1900 years ago the world's redemption took place . . . and was accompanied by the testament of the Redeemer,

expressed in extraordinary and quite remarkable words,
"Simon, son of John . . . feed my lambs . . . feed my
sheep." This is the basis on which everything is built. . . .
It is true, the choir of bishops of the whole world will cry:
*We also are bishops, while at Rome there is only one
bishop!* But this cry is ill-advised, for it is obvious from
the Gospel of Saint John, which is so profound and so
full of mystery in the last chapter, that everything has
been entrusted to Peter, to him alone, and in a quite extraordinary way. . . . The Pope is the rock on which all
rests; he feeds all the lambs, and apart from him everything is mere words. . . . The Pope is infallible not as
Pius or Leo, nor in his capacity as this man or that, but
in virtue of his dignity and office, in his mission and
apostolate, *ex cathedra.* . . . The Slavophils cry: *We are
the universal Church, Khomiakov and Samarin, or at least
the Holy Synod.* But the Pope can open the last chapter
of Saint John and read them that "my sheep" were entrusted to Simon Peter in person. Against these words of
the Redeemer subsequent events in the Church can avail
nothing. These words are special, marvelous, and occur-
ring at the end of the fourth and most mysterious Gospel,
are pronounced like a final testament. . . .

By entrusting his lambs and sheep personally and ex-
clusively to Peter, the Savior by this very fact eliminated
any notion of a collectivity in his Church. . . . *It has
pleased the Holy Ghost and us,* Acts, XV, 28, or, It has
pleased the Holy Ghost and me; does this not amount to
the same thing? Here, neither the *me* nor the *us* has any
importance; what is important is the Holy Ghost, who
speaks through many tongues or by a single tongue, by a
council or by the Pope. We might as well be completely
skeptical and defy not only the Pope but the council, and
say that the Holy Ghost is only mentioned for the sake
of appearances; in reality it is *we,* who are present—in
numbers, discussing, elucidating the truth, limiting each
other, spying on and observing each other—who are infallible, as opposed to the Pope who is *only one person*

and might invent goodness knows what mischief! The
Pope also takes counsel and studies matters . . . But at
the decisive moment when he speaks *ex cathedra,* Pius
and Leo fade into the background; it is the office, the role
of apostle, the Holy Ghost, which is there.

To anyone who has grasped the divine meaning of the
promise of Jesus it will seem useless to attempt to explain the presiding role of the Roman church in the
course of history by natural reasons. Rosanov continues:

This infallibility, which became a reality in the West,
remained a weak tentative thing in the East, as we might
expect, granted the precise meaning of the words of Jesus,
Feed my sheep. . . . As a result, there is an extraordinary feeling of irritation in the East against the West
. . . Byzantium whispered in the ear of Russia that Catholics are not even Christians. . . .

The psychology is everywhere the same—at Rome, Con-
stantinople, St. Petersburg, Kalouga or Toula. Only it is
not everywhere providential; it sometimes failed. It did
not succeed, except there where it was providential:
Feed my lambs . . . feed my sheep . . . feed my sheep,
repeated three times.

Like Soloviev, and like ourselves, Rosanov, although
he preferred to remain a member of the Orthodox
Church, also understood that the Gospel prophecy is the
true cause of the secular role of the papacy; and that,
conversely, the secular role of the papacy explains in our
opinion the mysterious meaning of the Gospel prophecy.
He saw no vicious circle there.

12

THE PRINCIPLE OF SUCCESSION
ACCORDING TO PROFESSOR CULLMANN

1. WHEN HE ARRIVES AT ROME PETER IS NO LONGER HEAD
   OF THE UNIVERSAL CHURCH. SOME SUITABLE EXPLANA-
   TION MUST THEREFORE BE FOUND FOR THE ACTUAL PRE-
   SIDING ROLE OF THE CHURCH OF ROME FROM THE EAR-
   LIEST TIMES

In the view of Prof. Cullmann Jesus reckons only with
a short period of time ". . . between his resurrection
and return," [1] and could therefore only confer on Peter
a temporary power for governing the church of Jerusalem during its first years. When Peter arrives in Rome,
he has already been deprived of the power of the keys:

> He exercised leadership over the entire Church only at
> the beginning of the Jerusalem church and thereby at the
> beginning of the whole Church. Then he carries out the
> missionary phase of his apostolic office, and does so in

[1] Cullmann, *Peter, Disciple, Apostle, Martyr*, p. 201.

the service of the Jewish Christian church of Jerusalem, whose leadership is in other hands.[2]

It is therefore completely impossible for him to transmit to any successors a power which he only exercised for a brief time, and which he has not enjoyed for quite some time. If the church of Rome occupies a position of pre-eminence from the second and third centuries on, the reason for this must be sought elsewhere:

> The secular historian, indeed, explains that pre-eminent position by the purely "immanent" consideration that Rome was the chief city of the Roman empire, so that the Christian church located there naturally and necessarily attained a special dignity. This reason certainly did play a strongly contributory role. In addition, the theologian will discover factors within the Church, grounded in the situation at that time, and with Ignatius of Antioch he may recognize that the Roman church of that time has also a "pre-eminence in love." [3]

But this pre-eminence is purely an accidental quality.

> But even if we wish to speak here of a divinely intended *development* in the history of the Church of Christ, it does not follow from this that this historical role is a sign that it is a divinely intended *norm* for the leadership of the Church of all time.[4]

The norm divinely intended for the Church for all time may therefore differ from that of Jesus, who, let us not forget, ". . . scarcely reckons with a duration of millenniums . . . between his resurrection and return." [5]

2 Cullmann, *op. cit.*, p. 226.
3 *Ibid.*, p. 233.
4 *Ibid.*, p. 233.
5 *Ibid.*, p. 201.

2. THE VICIOUS CIRCLE IN WHICH CATHOLICS ARE SAID TO ARGUE

We now come to the vicious circle in which Catholics are said to argue:

> It is arguing in a circle, a *petitio principii,* to assert that since on the one hand the promise of Jesus to Peter exists, and on the other hand the fact exists that Rome exercised a primacy from a relatively early date, we therefore must conclude that this primacy rests on that promise, in such a way that it is the norm for all time. That this relation exists between Matthew, XVI, 17ff. and the pre-eminent position that Rome later occupied is precisely the thing that it is necessary to prove.[6]

We reject this sophistical line of reasoning. It would be a vicious circle to say: we justify our interpretation of the prophecy of Jesus by the role of the church of Rome; and we justify the role of the church of Rome by our interpretation of the prophecy of Jesus. But that is not the way our argument runs. We justify our interpretation of the prophecy of Jesus from the Gospel text itself. We believe that Jesus is God, that all power was given to him in heaven and on earth, that he is the Master of all that happens in time, and that he was not ignorant of the period of his Church, nor of the hour of his own return. We read his prophecy without feeling any need beforehand to dismember it, or without beginning by separating verse 19 on the power of the keys from verse 18 on the foundation of the Church. We find that in order to protect his Church against the attacks of the city of evil Jesus founds it structurally, vertically, and as far as its

[6] Cullmann, *op. cit.,* p. 235.

continued existence in the present is concerned, on Peter, to whom he gives the keys of his Kingdom, and to whom he entrusts his lambs and his sheep during his absence. The structural foundation of the Church will endure as long as the Church; if the person of Peter dies, the office of Peter will survive. We know this by respecting the unity of the passage and by attributing to the Gospel prophecy its fullest meaning. We also know that by interpreting it thus we are reading it according to the mind of the Church.

Thus, when we find the role of the Roman church emerging at the place where Peter died, we know that we have the correct explanation for this phenomenon. This explanation is of a spiritual, mystical, and divine nature; it would be a misinterpretation of the Gospel to forget this. We do not attempt to have recourse to any natural explanation, or to take into account the spiritual prestige of the Roman church resulting from the political situation of Rome in the pagan empire. The whole thing is much more simple, more profound, and more divine than that: we explain the actual presiding role of the Roman church in the same way that we explain the actual presiding role of Peter in the Acts of the Apostles, by the spiritual efficacy of the promise of Jesus.[7] Conversely, the primacy of the church of Rome in the world, as well as the primacy of Peter in the Acts of the Apostles, explains the promise of Jesus; everywhere and at all times the fulfillment of a prophecy explains the prophecy. Jesus constantly proves the nature of his mission by an

---

[7] We explain in the same way the monotheistic belief and prophetic utterances of the Old Law, by an appeal to divine efficacy, and not by natural or fortuitous causes.

appeal to the prophecies of the Old Testament, and he constantly explains the prophetic utterances of the Old Testament by his own mission. If there is any circle involved in that, it is not vicious, but divine.

13

THE EARLIEST HISTORICAL DOCUMENTS
REFERRING TO THE STAY OF PETER IN ROME

1. THE EARLIEST LITERARY SOURCES

Some of these may be noticed briefly in chronological order:

The First Epistle of Peter ends with these words: "The Church here in Babylon, united with you by God's election, sends you her greeting; so does my son, Mark" (I Peter, V, 13). Babylon here, and in Apocalypse, XVII, 5, etc., is a symbolical name for Rome. Peter is writing from there to the Christians of Asia Minor.

The Gospel of Saint John, XXI, 18-19, alludes to the martyrdom of Peter, but does not indicate the place where it occurred:

Jesus said to him, Feed my sheep. Believe me when I tell thee this; as a young man, thou wouldst gird thyself and walk where thou hadst the will to go, but when thou hast grown old, another shall gird thee, and carry thee where thou goest, not of thy own will. So much he told him, prophesying the death by which he was to glorify God.[1]

About 96 A.D. Pope Saint Clement warns the Corinthians to be on guard against jealousy, and cites as an example the tribulations of the apostles Peter and Paul:

Let us pass in review the good Apostles: a Peter, who through unmerited jealousy underwent not one or two, but many hardships and, after thus *giving testimony*, departed for the place of glory that was his due. Through jealousy and strife Paul demonstrated how to win the prize of patient endurance: seven times he was imprisoned; he was forced to leave and stoned; he preached in the East and the West; and, finally, he won the splendid renown which his faith has earned. He taught the right manner of life to the whole world, travelled as far as the Western boundary, and, when he had given testimony before the authorities, ended his earthly career and was taken up into the holy place as the greatest model of patient endurance.

These men who had led holy lives were joined by a great multitude of the elect that suffered numerous indignities and tortures through jealousy and thus became illustrious examples among us.[2]

The phrase "giving testimony" in the case of Peter and that of Paul means "dies a martyr's death." [3] It is natural

---

[1] Some think that the two witnesses slain by the Beast and mentioned in Apoc., XI, 3ff. may be Peter and Paul, but this is mere conjecture.

[2] St. Clement of Rome, "Epistle to the Corinthians," *The Epistles of St. Clement of Rome and St. Ignatius of Antioch* (Ancient Christian Writers, ed. J. Quasten & J. C. Plumpe, Vol. I [Westminster, Md.: The Newman Press,] 1946), 5, 3-7; 6, 1, p. 12.

[3] "The word *martyrein* for 'bear witness' is at least already on the way to becoming the technical term for witness by martyrdom." Cullmann, *Peter, Disciple, Apostle, Martyr*, p. 95.

to think that Clement is here referring to the martyrs of the Roman church.

Saint Ignatius of Antioch, who died about 110 A.D., wrote as follows to the Romans:

> Not like Peter and Paul do I issue any orders to you. They were Apostles, I am a convict; they were free, I am until this moment a slave. But once I have suffered, I shall become a freedman of Jesus Christ, and, united with Him, I shall rise a free man (Ignatius *To the Romans,* IV, 3).

This is the way the famous introduction to this letter runs: [4]

> Ignatius, also called Theophorus, to the Church that has found mercy in the transcendent Majesty of the Most High Father and of Jesus Christ, His only Son; the church by the will of Him who willed all things that exist, beloved and illuminated through the faith and love of Jesus Christ our God; which also presides in the chief place of the Roman territory; a church worthy of God, worthy of honor, worthy of felicitation, worthy of praise, worthy of success, worthy of sanctification, and presiding in love, maintaining the law of Christ, and bearer of the Father's name: her do I therefore salute in the name of Jesus Christ, the Son of the Father. Heartiest good wishes for unimpaired joy in Jesus Christ our God.

Such is the honor and esteem which the Roman church enjoys in Eastern eyes because of the role of its two apostles.

[4] (Monsignor Journet quotes a version of this letter taken from O. Perler, "Ignatius von Antiochien und die römische Christengemeinde," *Divus Thomas* (Fribourg, 1944), pp. 413-451, and comments: "the writer [Perler] shows that this letter tacitly but obviously refers to the epistle of Pope Saint Clement to the Corinthians previously mentioned." The translation given here, similar to Msgr. Journet's version, is to be found in *The Epistles of St. Clement of Rome and St. Ignatius of Antioch,* p. 80. Translator's note.)

124

Saint Irenaeus, between 180 and 190 A.D., declares
that Matthew wrote his Gospel in Hebrew ". . . while
Peter and Paul were preaching at Rome and founding
the church there. After their death Mark, the disciple
and interpreter of Peter, also handed on to us in writing
the preaching of Peter . . ." [5]

And now we come to the important text in which Irenaeus, unable to list the various successions in all the
churches, concentrates his attention on

the very great Church, the very ancient and universally
known Church, founded and organized at Rome by the
two most glorious apostles, Peter and Paul.[6]

We shall show that the tradition which has come down
to it from the apostles, and the faith which is so renowned
throughout the world (Rom., I, 8), have come down to
us through a succession of bishops. This will put to confusion all those who in whatever manner, whether through
self-pleasing, vain-glory, blindness, or perverse judgment,
form unlawful gatherings. . . .

For every Church ought necessarily to agree with this
Church, on account of the pre-eminent authority of its
foundation [*propter potentiorem principalitatem*],[7] that
is, the faithful who come from everywhere [*hoc est eos
qui sunt undique fideles*], in as much as in this Church
the tradition which comes from the apostles has been preserved continuously by those who come from everywhere
[*ab his qui sunt undique*].[8]

[5] St. Irenaeus, *Adversus haereses*, III, 1, 1.
[6] *Ibid.*, III, 3, 2.
[7] In the absence of the Greek text we can only surmise what the meaning of this phrase is from the context. For the various attempts to
translate it, see Sagnard, *Contre les hérésies*, pp. 103-107, 414-423.
[8] Irenaeus, *op. cit.*, III, 3, 2. *Ab his qui sunt undique* refers to the
faithful from all parts who are gathered together in the unity of the
tradition which comes from the apostles.

After having thus founded and built the Church, the blessed apostles handed on the charge of the episcopate to Linus; Paul makes mention of this Linus in his letters to Timothy, II Tim., IV, 21. Anacletus succeeded him. After him in the third place from the apostles the episcopate fell to Clement. He had seen the apostles themselves and had been in touch with them; their preaching still sounded in his ears, their tradition was still before his eyes. . . . In the time of Clement a serious discussion arose with the brethren at Corinth; the Church of Rome on that occasion addressed a very important letter to the Corinthians in an attempt to conciliate them in peace, to arouse their faith, and to announce to them the tradition which it had recently received from the apostles. . . . All those who wish may thus know the tradition of the Church, since this letter is older than the present promoters of heresy. . . . This Clement was succeeded by Evaristus; Evaristus by Alexander; then in the sixth place from the apostles Sixtus was installed; after him Telesphorus, who also suffered a glorious martyr's death; then Hyginus; then Pius; after him Anicetus; Soter having succeeded Anicetus, Eleutherius is now the one to whom has fallen the episcopate, in the twelfth place from the apostles. It is in this order and in this line of succession that the tradition which has come down in the Church from the time of the apostles, and the preaching of the truth, have come down to our own day.[9]

The Canon of Muratori, dated about 200 A.D., states that Saint Luke recounted what had actually taken place under his eyes in the Acts of the Apostles, hence his "omission of the passion of Peter."

Also about 200 A.D., the presbyter Gaius wrote: "But I can point out the trophies [*tropaia*] of the apostles. For if you will go to the Vatican or to the Ostian Way you

[9] Irenaeus, *op. cit.*, III, 3, 3. See above pages 58, and 84.

will find the trophies of those who founded this Church." [10]

All these texts, which are very familiar to Prof. Cullmann and discussed by him with a great deal of learning, can be studied in the light of historical criticism alone. In such case they give rise to numerous and interesting questions. They lead Prof. Cullmann to the following conclusion:

> It is sufficient to let us *include the martyrdom of Peter in Rome in our final historical picture of the early Church, as a fact which is relatively though not absolutely assured.* We accept it, however, with the self-evident caution that we have to use concerning many other facts of antiquity that are universally accepted as historical. Were we to demand for all facts of ancient history a greater degree of probability, we should have to strike from our history books a large proportion of their contents.[11]

But these documents can also be read in another light. We can see in them the faint and disconnected imprint left at random on the sands of time by the great living mystery of the Church, which divinely continues the mystery of the redemptive Incarnation. Then and then only do these poor texts seem to possess once again their real sublime meaning and hidden relationship, in the light which comes from above; something of the same sort happens when we set out to re-read the narrative of the Synoptic Gospels in the light of the prologue to Saint John's Gospel. It was thus, we can be sure, that Irenaeus looked at the history of the Church. It is useless to find fault with him for seeing in the apostle Paul one of the

10 This statement is preserved in Eusebius, *Hist. eccles.*, II, 25, 7; translated by K. Lake (Loeb Library), p. 183.

11 Cullmann, *op. cit.*, p. 114.

founders of the church of Rome.[12] Could apostles, such
as Peter and Paul, make an appearance in any already
existing church without seeming to be what the sun is
to the day?

2. THE VATICAN EXCAVATIONS

What are the results of the excavations which have recently been carried on at the Vatican, very briefly?

If Constantine chose to build a basilica to the apostle
Peter, about the year 333 A.D., on a piece of ground
which presented enormous difficulties for his architects
because of the steep gradient of the locality and because
it was already occupied by a pagan cemetery which had
to be demolished, it must have been because he wished
to honor a tradition which fixed the location of the apostle's tomb at this very spot.

The excavations under the high altar of St. Peter's basilica have brought to light a small funerary monument
with a semi-cylindrical niche, which can be dated fairly
accurately, and which appears to have been the trophy,
tropaion, of Peter, which the presbyter Gaius offered to
show at the Vatican about the year 200 A.D.[13]

What does the word trophy signify? As used by Gaius

[12] Cullmann, *op. cit.,* p. 116.
[13] "Provisionally, however—though not at all with certainty—we may
assert, for the reasons given, that the 'trophy' of Gaius appears to
have been found." Cullmann, *op. cit.,* p. 146. (The results of the
excavations were given to the world in *Esplorazioni sotto la Con-
fessione di San Pietro in Vaticano,* 2 Vols. [Vatican, 1951], and
have been the subject of numerous articles and much discussion.
The best account of the significance of the excavations, from the
archaeological point of view, is that of J. M. C. Toynbee, "The
Shrine of St. Peter and its Setting," *Journal of Roman Studies,* XLIII
[1953], p. 1ff.—Translator's note.)

it seems to mean a tomb, the tomb of the apostle. Yet this meaning of the word trophy is unusual. Perhaps it only means a cenotaph. We are therefore faced with two alternatives: either the trophy is a simple monument which marked the approximate place where it was thought at this date that the tomb of the apostle was; or the trophy is a tomb and perhaps contained in its niche an urn with certain relics of the apostle Peter, which have now disappeared.

Erik Peterson, whose study we are summarizing [14] here, personally favors the first alternative. The trophy is thought to be older than the time when the cult of the martyrs was celebrated at Rome. [15] No rows of benches for the worshippers were found, as in the catacombs of San Sebastiano. It might be a cenotaph, or commemorative monument, erected on the spot where an ancient tradition held that the tomb of Peter was located.

Peterson presents his opinions with a great deal of modesty, and ends his article by saying that they will perhaps seem too tentative to those who think that archaeology has now resolved all the secrets concerning the tomb of Peter. We have already pointed out, however, that between the simple historical certainty that Peter came to Rome and died there and the certainty by which we believe according to divine faith that Peter established his see in Rome, there is a world of difference. Let us conclude, therefore, by agreeing with Peter-

---

[14] E. Peterson, "Über das Petrusgrab," *Schweizer Rundschau* (Sept., 1952), pp. 326-331.

[15] That is, before 200 A.D. The letter of the Church of Smyrna on the *Martyrdom of Polycarp* is the oldest written document which shows that Christians in the East were interested in venerating the relics of the martyrs (Chap. XVII). Polycarp died in 155, not in 177. See Sagnard, *Contre les hérésies*, III, p. 10.

son that in matters of this sort Christians should never ignore the claims of supernatural faith, but that archaeology may sometimes help in a very striking way to establish the credibility of this faith.

CONCLUSION

It may be worth while to summarize here the principal stages of Prof. Cullmann's argument.

"Jesus scarcely reckons with a duration of millenniums, but he does assume that there will be a rather brief period of time between his resurrection and return."

The words of Jesus at the end of Matthew: "All authority in heaven and on earth has been given to me; you, therefore, must go out, making disciples of *all nations* . . . *And behold I am with you all through the days that are coming, until the consummation of the world*," are valid only for the past.

The passage of John, XVII, in which Jesus prays for those who will believe in him through the *word* of the apostles, simply means that Jesus is praying for those who will believe in him through the writings of the apostles.

Jesus is concerned with an immediate situation when he says to Peter: "Thou art Rock and on this rock I will build my Church." These words definitely cannot be interpreted as meaning that Peter will found the Church in the sense that a *rock* or *foundation* serves to support the weight of a building, that is *structurally*, and as far as its continued existence is concerned.

This passage means that Peter will found the Church the way a *workman* lays the foundation of a building, that is, in a purely incidental sense as far as its existence in the past is concerned. The workman may die, but the building remains. His role as founder cannot be handed on.

The rock on which the Church will be founded will already have disappeared, when the great assaults of the powers of hell will be made against it.

It is logical, therefore, in interpreting Matthew XVI, to separate verse 18, which supposedly refers to a temporary foundation, from verse 19, which certainly speaks of a permanent power of the keys, rather than to explain the one with reference to the other.

Since the function of founding the Church in the manner of a workman who lays the foundations is common to all the apostles, the power of Peter does not differ essentially from the power of the other apostles.

There can be no thought of distinguishing the apostles according to John XXI, 15-17, as apostles, and as sheep of Christ who have been entrusted to Peter as sole pastor. There is no distinction between the apostolic privilege common to all the apostles, and the transapostolic privilege belonging to Peter, which makes them unequal.

Peter is superior to the other apostles because he first

saw the Risen Christ—and *not vice versa.* His purely accidental superiority is due to his "chronological pre-eminence."

Because of this chronological pre-eminence he assumes the leadership of the church at Jerusalem in the beginning, which at that time comprised the universal Church. "Peter, with the other apostles, forms the foundation, and yet at the same time constitutes the rock within the foundation." [1]

This momentary pre-eminence fully justifies the promises which make Peter the foundation which supports the Church against the assaults of hell, the steward of the Kingdom of Christ, and the sole pastor of his lambs and his sheep.

It also enables all Protestant churches to declare that they are truly founded on Peter.

Peter is quickly supplanted by James as the head of the church at Jerusalem; henceforth there can be no question of the former as head of the universal Church.

Opposed to the group of churches with James at the head is the group of churches headed by Paul. "Thus there occurred even in Primitive Christianity a decisive church split." The apostles could not bridge their differences, "which concerned a *central point,* that is, the conception of grace."

Peter became subordinate to James, and "must accept a rebuke" from Paul.

When Peter arrives in Rome, he has long ceased to possess the power of the keys, which Jesus had promised him, and to be the head of the universal Church.

He dies a martyr's death at Rome without having anything to bequeath to his successors.

[1] Cullmann, *Peter, Disciple, Apostle Martyr,* p. 218.

The effective presiding role of the Roman church from the second century on, as a consequence, can be explained by political reasons, or merely accidental ones.

Let us meditate on these nineteen propositions which give us a sufficient idea of the theses of Prof. Cullmann. Let us meditate especially on the fact that he begins by asserting the authenticity of the Gospel text, but then, in order to avoid giving it the Catholic interpretation of *Tu es Petrus*, consigns the apostolic Church itself, which has scarcely emerged from the hands of Christ and is still enlightened by the graces of Pentecost, to a "decisive church split." Let anyone compare his laborious historical reconstruction with the profound coherence of the Catholic interpretation and the conclusion inevitably seems to be that he has failed in his attempt. It is difficult not to think once again of the saying of Chesterton: "In place of a supernatural history which is likely, they give us natural stories which are unlikely."

Once again, I should like to say that it is not Prof. Cullmann's qualifications as a scholar or historian which are being questioned here. It is rather a question of something much more subtle, the over-all point of view which these qualifications are intended to serve. When we see such labor, erudition, patience and integrity result in what we can only characterize as a rationalization of the gospel message, how can we avoid being saddened by the prospect? It seems that all human efforts to illuminate divine truth in such cases as this are doomed in advance to be ineffectual. There is no other recourse than prayer. We are reminded of Saint Paul who could not succeed in making the children of Israel understand that all the prophecies they knew by heart and cherished only served to announce Jesus and his

Kingdom whom they continued to misunderstand—and who accordingly came to realize that only the divine mercy could dispel this misunderstanding:

> But in spite of that, dullness has crept over their senses, and to this day the reading of the old law is muffled with the same veil; no revelation tells them that it has been abrogated in Christ. To this day, I say, when the law of Moses is read out, a veil hangs over their hearts. There must be a turning to the Lord first, and then the veil will be taken away (II Cor., III, 14-16).

We have just spoken of a fatal misunderstanding, not of bad faith.

Among the children of Israel who today cherish the prophecies without understanding the true meaning, many are able to find a place in their hearts for that initial Christlike charity which the Holy Ghost diffuses so mysteriously throughout the world, without knowing it as such by this name. Thenceforth, they are already members, albeit in an obscure, initial and imperfect way, of this true Christ, whom their minds continue to misunderstand because of some misconception for which they are not responsible.

What we have just said about belonging to Christ in an obscure sort of way through charity, can also be said, on a different level, about acceptance of the primacy of Peter.

> Acceptance of the primacy of Peter, like membership in Christ and in the Church, can be veiled and tendentious, yet saving. It may be that a person of good faith feels his conscience revolt against the doctrine of the primacy of Peter. Because of a series of misunderstandings which have accumulated through the centuries and which claim him as a victim through no fault of his own, this doctrine may seem to him today not what it really is, the testament

of love which Christ left his Church when he organized
his sheep before ascending into heaven, but as a recru-
descence of paganism, a sacrilegious thing, and an offence
against the holiness of God and his Gospel. What must
the Catholic theologian say to this? He will say that if a
person is truly sincere and humble in his heart, receptive
of the divine graces which secretly visit him and sub-
missive without reservation to the designs of God and
Christ, he has already accepted in its source and completely a doctrine which he denies directly and formally
as to content, only because he does not perceive its divine
origin.

It can come to pass, however, that this person finds that
erroneous views, which had hitherto seemed to be insurmountable, gradually tend to vanish under the influence of divine grace. This is what happened to Newman,
Soloviev, and to countless others. Then he will hear those
words of Christ to Peter sound of their own accord in the
bottom of his heart with a divine insistence and with a
meaning which he never suspected was there before:
Feed my sheep. When that happens, the Catholic definition of the Roman primacy will cease to be a scandal for
him, and will become as clear as the light of day.[2]

[2] Journet, *L'Eglise du Verbe incarné*, II, p. 1096.

140

CULLMANN, OSCAR (*Continued*)
on Christ in the Church, 45–46
on chronological founding of the Church, 75–78
on Church and teaching office, 44–47
on Church continuity, 55–56
on James as head of the Church, 87–89
on Kingdom of God, 45
on martyrdom of St. Peter, 126
on mission of the Apostles, 44–45
on powers of St. Peter, not transapostolic, 85–87
on privilege of St. Peter, 73–102
on promise made to Peter by Jesus, 78–80
on schism in the Church, 97–102
on transapostolic power of founding of the Church, 75–78
Peter, Disciple, Apostle, Martyr, summary, 1–7

DISCIPLES, perpetuation of Christ's priesthood and kingship in, 16

EUCHARIST
in mnemic concept of Christianity, 19–20
perpetuation of Christ's priesthood and kingship, 15–17
realism in, Fr. de Lubac on, 26–27

EXCAVATIONS, in the Vatican, 127–129, 127n

FAITH
Catholicism on, 107–109
in mnemic concept of Christianity, 21
norm
    Catholic view, 54
    Protestant view, 54

GARDEIL, AMBROISE, O.P., on exegetical method, 3

GRACE
apostolic, Cullmann on, 50–52
in mnemic concept of Christianity, 21

HADES. *See* Hell

HELL, place of punishment, 61n

HOLINESS, of Christ, perpetuation, 17–18

HOLY EUCHARIST. *See* Eucharist

HOLY SCRIPTURE. *See* Bible

IGNATIUS OF ANTIOCH, ST., on St. Peter's stay in Rome, 123